PRAISE FOR ROBERT BUCKLEY

From *"The Power of ESG Investing:"*

For anyone wanting to know more about ESG investing, and why considering ESG factors is important, this book is a must read! Well written & chapter summaries make the information easy to digest.

— R MURRELL

I recently read *"The Power of ESG Investing"* and was thoroughly impressed. The authors do an excellent job of explaining the concept of Environmental, Social, and Governance (ESG) investing and its growing significance in the investment world. The book provides a clear and concise overview of the key ESG factors to consider when making investment decisions, along with practical advice for incorporating ESG considerations into an investment strategy ... It's an invaluable resource for anyone looking to make a positive impact while also potentially enhancing returns.

— MARK VAN

The author does an excellent job of explaining complex financial concepts in a clear and accessible manner, making it an ideal resource for both seasoned investors and those new to the world of investing.

— STOICPRENEUR

THE POWER OF SUSTAINABLE INVESTING

THE POWER OF SUSTAINABLE INVESTING

GENERATE FINANCIAL RETURNS AND MAKE RESPONSIBLE AND ETHICAL DECISIONS WITH ESG AND IMPACT INVESTING COMBINED (2-IN-1 COLLECTION)

SOCIALLY RESPONSIBLE INVESTING

ROBERT BUCKLEY

Book
Bound Studios

To my family for their unwavering support and encouragement throughout the writing of this book. And to my mentor and friend Justina, whose guidance and wisdom have been invaluable in shaping my understanding of ESG and impact investing.

Investing is not only about making money, it's also about making a difference.

— JACQUELINE NOVOGRATZ

CONTENTS

From the Author xvii

THE POWER OF ESG INVESTING

Introduction 3

1. ENVIRONMENTAL CONSIDERATIONS IN ESG INVESTING 9
   - Climate Change and Carbon Emissions 9
   - Renewable Energy and Resource Efficiency 11
   - Biodiversity and Habitat Preservation 12
   - Water Management and Pollution Control 14
   - Waste Management and Recycling Programs 15
   - Chapter Summary 17
2. SOCIAL CONSIDERATIONS IN ESG INVESTING 19
   - Labor and Human Rights 19
   - Community Engagement and Development 21
   - Diversity, Equity, and Inclusion 22
   - Product Safety and Consumer Protection 23
   - Chapter Summary 25
3. GOVERNANCE CONSIDERATIONS IN ESG INVESTING 27
   - Corporate Governance and Executive Compensation 27
   - Transparency and Disclosure 30
   - Political Lobbying and Advocacy 31
   - Anti-Corruption and Bribery Policies 32
   - Tax Transparency and Responsible Tax Practices 33
   - Chapter Summary 35
4. INTEGRATING ESG CONSIDERATIONS INTO INVESTMENT STRATEGY 37
   - Screening and Exclusion 37
   - Active Ownership and Engagement 39
   - Impact Investing 40
   - Chapter Summary 41

5. MEASURING AND EVALUATING ESG PERFORMANCE 43
ESG Ratings and Indices 43
Assessing Company-Specific ESG Data 44
The Limitations and Challenges of ESG Measurement 45
Chapter Summary 47

6. THE ROLE OF REGULATORS AND GOVERNMENT IN ESG INVESTING 49
The Regulatory Framework for ESG Investing 49
Government Policies and Initiatives Promoting ESG Investing 50
The Influence of Global Regulatory Developments on ESG Investing 51
Chapter Summary 53

7. ESG INVESTING AND FINANCIAL PERFORMANCE 55
The Historical and Current Research on the Relationship Between ESG and Financial Performance 55
The Potential Risks and Benefits of ESG Investing for Investors 57
The Role of Active Management in ESG Investing 58
Chapter Summary 59

8. ESG INVESTING IN PRACTICE 61
Case Studies of Successful ESG Investing Strategies 61
Best Practices for Implementing ESG Investing 67
The Role of Investors, Asset Managers, and Other Stakeholders in Advancing ESG Investing 73
Chapter Summary 74

Epilogue 77

THE POWER OF IMPACT INVESTING

Introduction 83

1. UNDERSTANDING IMPACT INVESTING 89
Principles of Impact Investing 90
Impact Measurement and Evaluation 91
Risks and Challenges of Impact Investing 92
Impact Investing vs. Traditional Investing 94

Impact Investing in Developing Countries 95
Chapter Summary 96

2. IMPACT INVESTING STRATEGIES 97
Socially Responsible Investing 98
Environmental, Social, and Governance (ESG) Investing 99
Community Investing 99
Microfinance 100
Impact Bonds 100
Chapter Summary 101

3. IMPACT INVESTING SECTORS 103
Education 104
Healthcare 105
Renewable Energy 105
Agriculture 106
Affordable Housing 107
Chapter Summary 107

4. IMPACT INVESTING IN ACTION 109
Case Studies of Successful Impact Investments 110
Impact Investing in the Public Sector 111
Impact Investing in the Private Sector 111
Impact Investing in Philanthropy 112
Impact Investing in the Nonprofit Sector 112
Chapter Summary 113

5. IMPACT INVESTING AND SUSTAINABLE DEVELOPMENT GOALS 115
Overview of Sustainable Development Goals 116
SDG 1: No Poverty 116
SDG 2: Zero Hunger 117
SDG 3: Good Health and Well-being 117
SDG 4: Quality Education 117
Chapter Summary 118

6. IMPACT INVESTING AND SUSTAINABLE DEVELOPMENT GOALS (CONT.) 121
SDG 5: Gender Equality 122
SDG 6: Clean Water and Sanitation 123
SDG 7: Affordable and Clean Energy 124
SDG 8: Decent Work and Economic Growth 125

SDG 9: Industry, Innovation, and Infrastructure 126
Chapter Summary 127

7. IMPACT INVESTING AND SUSTAINABLE DEVELOPMENT GOALS (CONT.) 129
SDG 10: Reduced Inequalities 130
SDG 11: Sustainable Cities and Communities 131
SDG 12: Responsible Consumption and Production 131
SDG 13: Climate Action 132
SDG 14: Life Below Water 132
Chapter Summary 133

8. IMPACT INVESTING AND SUSTAINABLE DEVELOPMENT GOALS (CONT.) 135
SDG 15: Life on Land 136
SDG 16: Peace, Justice, and Strong Institutions 137
SDG 17: Partnerships for the Goals 138
Impact Investing and the Future of Sustainable Development 139
Impact Investing and the Role of Governments 140
Chapter Summary 141

9. IMPACT INVESTING AND SOCIAL ENTREPRENEURSHIP 143
Definition of Social Entrepreneurship 144
Social Entrepreneurship and Impact Investing 145
Social Entrepreneurship Models 146
Social Entrepreneurship and Innovation 147
Social Entrepreneurship and Sustainability 148
Chapter Summary 149

10. IMPACT INVESTING AND CORPORATE SOCIAL RESPONSIBILITY 151
Definition of Corporate Social Responsibility 152
Corporate Social Responsibility and Impact Investing 152
Corporate Social Responsibility Models 153
Corporate Social Responsibility and Innovation 154
Corporate Social Responsibility and Sustainability 155
Chapter Summary 157

11. IMPACT INVESTING AND ETHICAL INVESTING 159
Definition of Ethical Investing 160
Ethical Investing and Impact Investing 160

Ethical Investing Models 161
Ethical Investing and Innovation 162
Ethical Investing and Sustainability 163
Chapter Summary 164

12. IMPACT INVESTING AND THE FUTURE OF INVESTING 167
Trends in Impact Investing 168
Impact Investing and the Global Economy 169
Impact Investing and the Financial Industry 169
Impact Investing and the Role of Investors 170
Impact Investing and the Role of Consumers 171
Chapter Summary 172

13. IMPACT INVESTING RESOURCES 173
Impact Investing Organizations 174
Impact Investing Publications: 175
Impact Investing Conferences and Events 176
Impact Investing Networks and Communities: 177
Impact Investing Tools and Resources: 178
Chapter Summary 179

Epilogue 181

Acknowledgments 183
About the Author 185
From the Author 187

THE POWER OF ESG INVESTING

NAVIGATING ENVIRONMENTAL, SOCIAL, AND GOVERNANCE FACTORS FOR SUSTAINABLE AND RESPONSIBLE INVESTING

INTRODUCTION

Environmental, social, and governance (ESG) investing has gained significant attention in recent years as more investors have become interested in aligning their investments with their values. ESG investing is a type of investing that incorporates consideration of a company's environmental, social, and governance practices and performance into investment decisions. The purpose of this chapter is to provide an overview of ESG investing, including its definition, the growing popularity of ESG investing, and the goals and benefits of incorporating ESG considerations into investment decisions. We will also explore the various environmental, social, and governance considerations that investors should consider when evaluating a company's ESG practices and performance. This chapter aims to provide a comprehensive introduction to ESG investing, setting the stage for a deeper dive into the following topic in the subsequent chapters.

Definition of ESG Investing

ESG investing, or environmental, social, and governance investing, is a type of investment strategy that incorporates consideration of a company's environmental, social, and governance practices and performance into investment decisions. Environmental factors include a company's environmental impact, such as its carbon footprint and approach to natural resources management. Social factors include a company's labor practices, community engagement, and its approach to diversity, equity, and inclusion. Governance factors include a company's management structure, board composition, executive compensation, lobbying approach, advocacy, and transparency. ESG investing is also known as sustainable, responsible, or impact investing.

ESG investing involves evaluating a company's impact on the environment, its treatment of employees, customers, and communities, and how it manages and governs itself. This type of investing is gaining popularity among investors who want to align their investments with their values and **contribute to a more sustainable future.** ESG investors are looking to achieve financial returns while promoting positive social and environmental change by investing in companies committed to sustainable business practices. By considering a company's ESG practices and performance, investors can identify potential risks and opportunities that may not be reflected in traditional financial analysis. Additionally, ESG investing can help align investors' values with their investments, promote greater corporate accountability and transparency, and contribute to developing a more sustainable global economy.

The Growing Popularity of ESG Investing

In recent years, ESG investing has gained significant attention and popularity among investors, becoming one of the fastest-growing investment trends. This is due to the growing awareness of the importance of sustainable practices and investors' role in promoting positive social and environmental change. The increasing focus on climate change and environmental sustainability, as well as the growing awareness of social and governance issues, has led many investors to re-evaluate their investment strategies and consider the impact of their investments on the world around them.

Several factors have contributed to the growing popularity of ESG investing. One of the main drivers has been the increasing awareness of the urgent need for action on climate change and environmental sustainability. As the impacts of climate change become more severe and widespread, investors are increasingly recognizing the need to invest in companies that are taking action to reduce their carbon footprint and promote sustainable resource management.

Another factor has been the growing awareness of social and governance issues, such as labor practices, community engagement, and diversity and inclusion. Investors are becoming increasingly concerned about the companies' social and governance practices. As a result, they are looking for ways to invest in companies that promote positive social and environmental outcomes.

In addition to these external factors, there has also been a growing body of research that demonstrates the potential financial benefits of ESG investing. For example, several studies have shown that companies with strong ESG practices tend to have better management, lower risk, and higher long-term returns. This has led many investors to re-evaluate their investment strategies and consider the impact of their investments on the world around them.

The growing popularity of ESG investing has also been reflected in the **growing number of ESG-focused investment products and services.** For example, increasing numbers of asset managers and investment companies are launching ESG-focused funds and products, and many index providers are developing ESG-focused indices and benchmarks. This has made it easier for investors to access ESG-focused investment opportunities, further driving the popularity of ESG investing.

The Goals and Benefits of ESG Investing

The primary goal of ESG (environmental, social, and governance) investing is to achieve financial returns while promoting positive social and environmental change. This approach to investing seeks to identify companies with strong financial performance and demonstrate a commitment to sustainable business practices. By considering a company's ESG practices and performance, investors can identify potential risks and opportunities that may not be reflected in traditional financial analysis. Additionally, ESG investing can help align investors' values with their investments, promote greater corporate accountability and transparency, and contribute to developing a more sustainable global economy.

The benefits of ESG investing are numerous. One of the main benefits is that companies with strong ESG practices tend to have better management and lower risk, which can result in **higher long-term returns**. This is because companies with a strong commitment to sustainable business practices are more likely to have better governance, more transparent operations, and more efficient use of resources, which can lead to long-term financial performance.

ESG investing can also help to mitigate risks associated with climate change, labor practices, and other social and environmental issues. For example, investing in companies committed to reducing their carbon footprint and promoting sustainable resource management can help mitigate the financial risks associated with climate change. Similarly, investing in companies with strong labor practices and promoting diversity and inclusion can help mitigate the risks associated with social and governance issues.

ESG investing can also promote the development of more sustainable business practices. Investing in companies committed to sustainable business practices can create a financial incentive to continue improving their environmental, social, and governance practices. Additionally, by engaging with companies on ESG issues, investors can help promote greater corporate accountability and transparency, leading to more sustainable business practices.

All in all, ESG investing is a powerful tool that can help investors achieve financial returns while promoting positive social and environmental change. By considering a company's ESG practices and performance, investors can identify potential risks and opportunities that may not be reflected in traditional financial analysis, align their values with their investments, promote greater corporate accountability and transparency, and contribute to developing a more sustainable global economy.

In conclusion, ESG investing is a rapidly growing trend in the investment world, driven by increasing awareness of the importance of sustainable practices and investors' role in promoting positive social and environmental change. By considering a company's ESG practices and performance, investors can identify potential risks and opportunities that may not be reflected in traditional financial analysis. Additionally, ESG investing can help align investors' values with their investments, promote greater corporate accountability and transparency, and contribute to developing a more sustainable global economy. In the next chapter, we will delve deeper into environmental considerations in ESG investing, including climate change and baron emissions, renewable energy and resource efficiency, and biodiversity and habitat preservation.

1

ENVIRONMENTAL CONSIDERATIONS IN ESG INVESTING

This chapter will explore how environmental factors play a crucial role in socially responsible investing. We will delve into five topics that are particularly relevant in today's sustainable investing landscape: climate change and carbon emissions, renewable energy and resource efficiency, biodiversity and habitat preservation, water management, and pollution control, and waste management and recycling programs. We aim to comprehensively understand how these environmental factors impact investment decisions and how investors can use this knowledge to make informed and responsible choices. We hope this chapter will serve as a valuable resource for those interested in responsible investing and its impact on our planet.

Climate Change and Carbon Emissions

Climate change is one of our most significant environmental challenges, and it profoundly impacts the planet and the global economy. Burning fossil fuels, deforestation, and other human activities have increased greenhouse gas emissions, causing global temperatures to rise and resulting in more extreme weather events, rising sea levels, and other negative environmental impacts. As a result, climate change poses a significant risk to the global economy, and companies **must** take action to reduce their carbon footprint and mitigate the risks associated with climate change.

A tree with its roots firmly planted in the ground representing the foundation of ESG investing.

One of the key ways that companies can reduce their carbon footprint is by reducing their greenhouse gas emissions. Companies can achieve this through various methods, such as investing in renewable energy, implementing energy-efficient practices, and using clean technology. In addition, companies committed to reducing their greenhouse gas emissions are more likely to be sustainable in the long term and, therefore, are more attractive to ESG investors.

Another way to mitigate the risks associated with climate change is by investing in renewable energy and clean technology. Renewable energy sources such as solar, wind, and hydropower produce no emissions, and they help to reduce the use of fossil fuels, which are a major contributor to climate change. Clean technology, on the other hand, refers to technology that is designed to reduce environmental impact. Therefore, investing in companies developing and deploying renewable energy and clean technology can help mitigate the risks associated with climate change and promote sustainable development.

Lastly, ESG investors are increasingly looking to divest from companies that rely heavily on fossil fuels. As the world shifts towards cleaner energy sources, companies heavily dependent on fossil fuels are becoming more vulnerable to stranded assets, regulatory risks, and reputational risks. By divesting from these companies, investors can mitigate the risks associated with climate change and promote sustainable development.

In conclusion, climate change and carbon emissions are major environmental challenges that pose significant risks to the global economy. As a result, ESG investors are increasingly looking to invest in companies that are taking action to reduce their carbon footprint and mitigate the risks associated with climate change.

Renewable Energy and Resource Efficiency

The importance of utilizing renewable energy sources and implementing resource efficiency practices cannot be overstated when achieving sustainable development. Renewable energy, such as solar and wind power, does not generate harmful emissions and helps to reduce our dependence on fossil fuels, which are major contributors to climate change. On the other hand, resource efficiency involves sustainably using resources with minimal waste, which can greatly reduce the environmental impact of our actions, lower costs, and increase overall efficiency.

Companies committed to utilizing renewable energy sources and implementing resource efficiency practices are more likely to be **sustainable in the long term.** As a result, they are better positioned to be competitive in the future energy market. This has led to an increased interest from ESG investors in such companies, as they can provide benefits such as reduced risk, improved financial performance, and long-term sustainability.

By investing in companies that are actively working towards increasing renewable energy and resource efficiency, we can not only help to reduce the environmental impact of our actions but also benefit from the long-term sustainability of these companies. Therefore, individuals and organizations need to recognize the importance of renewable energy and resource efficiency in achieving sustainable development and take the necessary steps to promote and invest in these practices.

A majestic wind turbine stands tall against a brilliant sunset symbolizing the limitless power of renewable energy.

Biodiversity and Habitat Preservation

Biodiversity and habitat preservation are critical for maintaining the health and resilience of the planet's ecosystems. Biodiversity refers to the variety of life on Earth, including plants, animals, and microorganisms that make up the planet's ecosystems. Habitat preservation refers to protecting and preserving natural habitats, such as forests, wetlands, and oceans, which are critical for maintaining biodiversity and supporting the planet's ecosystems.

The loss of biodiversity and habitat destruction is a major environmental issue that poses significant risks to the planet's ecosystems. Habitat destruction and loss of biodiversity can lead to the extinction of species, loss of ecosystem services, and increased vulnerability to natural disasters and climate change. It is, therefore, important that companies take action to protect and preserve biodiversity and habitats.

ESG investors are increasingly looking to invest in businesses committed to biodiversity and habitat preservation. This can include investing in companies committed to sustainable resource management, such as companies working to reduce their impact on natural habitats and ecosystems. For example, companies that practice sustainable forestry, fishing, and mining are less likely to cause damage to natural habitats and ecosystems. As a result, they are more likely to be sustainable in the long term. Additionally, investing in companies working to preserve and protect natural habitats and biodiversity can help mitigate the risks associated with habitat destruction and loss of biodiversity.

Another way that companies can support biodiversity and habitat preservation is by investing in conservation and restoration projects. This can include investing in reforestation projects, wetland restoration, and other initiatives that help to protect and preserve biodiversity and habitats.

All in all, biodiversity and habitat preservation are critical for maintaining the health and resilience of the planet's ecosystems. As a result, ESG investors are increasingly looking to invest in companies committed to biodiversity and habitat preservation. Investing in companies committed to sustainable resource management, conservation, and restoration projects, and preserving and protecting natural habitats and biodiversity can help mitigate the risks associated with habitat destruction and loss of biodiversity and promote sustainable development.

Water Management and Pollution Control

Water management and pollution control are critical considerations for investing in environmental, social, and governance (ESG). As water is a **finite resource** and pollution can significantly negatively impact human health and the environment, companies that effectively manage and reduce their water usage and pollution can be considered more sustainable investments.

Water management involves the responsible use and conservation of water resources. This includes reducing water usage through efficient practices, implementing recycling and reuse systems, and protecting water sources from pollution. Companies with strong water management practices can reduce their environmental footprint and save on water procurement and treatment costs.

On the other hand, pollution control involves reducing the release of harmful substances into the environment, including water. This includes reducing the use of hazardous chemicals, implementing proper disposal methods for waste materials, and monitoring for and preventing spills and leaks. As a result, companies with strong pollution control practices can protect the environment and human health and reduce the risk of legal and reputational damage.

When evaluating companies for ESG investing, it is important to look at their water management and pollution control practices. This can include analyzing their water usage and conservation efforts, reviewing their environmental impact reports and sustainability goals, and assessing their compliance with relevant laws and regulations. It is also important to consider the company's industry, as certain industries may have a higher potential for water usage and pollution.

Investors can also consider investing in companies specializing in water management and pollution control technologies and services. These companies can provide solutions for other companies to improve their water management and pollution control practices. They can also benefit from increased demand for sustainable water management and pollution control solutions.

In conclusion, water management and pollution control are important considerations for ESG investing. Companies with strong water management and pollution control practices can be considered more sustainable investments. Investors can also consider investing in companies specializing in water management and pollution control technologies and services.

Waste Management and Recycling Programs

Waste management and recycling programs are crucial components of environmental, social, and governance (ESG) investing. These programs help protect the environment and generate economic and social benefits for communities and businesses.

Effective waste management and recycling programs involve the collection, transportation, and processing of waste materials in a manner that reduces their environmental impact. This can include reducing waste in landfills, increasing materials recycling, and finding new uses for waste products.

One key aspect of waste management and recycling programs is diverting waste from landfills. Landfills are a significant source of greenhouse gas emissions and can negatively impact air and water quality. By diverting waste from landfills through recycling and composting, we can greatly reduce the environmental impact of waste.

Another important aspect of these programs is the recycling of materials. Recycling conserves natural resources, reduces energy consumption and the need for new landfills, and can create jobs and economic benefits. In addition, many materials, such as paper, glass, and metal, can be recycled multiple times, making them a valuable resource.

Many companies are looking for innovative ways to use waste as a resource. This is commonly known as a circular economy. As a result, companies can benefit from cost savings, reduced waste, and improved environmental performance.

Furthermore, ESG investors should consider the environmental performance of companies in the waste management and recycling industry. They should assess the environmental impact of the company's operations, its compliance with environmental regulations, and efforts to reduce waste and promote recycling. Investors can also look for companies developing new technologies and processes to improve waste management and recycling.

A bustling city street lined with colorful recycling bins overflowing with paper, plastic, and glass.

Overall, waste management and recycling programs are important aspects of ESG investing. These programs can help to protect the environment, generate economic and social benefits, and create new business opportunities. ESG investors can support these programs by investing in companies committed to effective waste management and recycling practices and implementing circular economy strategies.

In conclusion, this chapter has highlighted the importance of considering environmental factors in ESG investing. From climate change and carbon emissions to waste management and recycling programs, we have explored how these factors play a crucial role in sustainable investing. We hope this chapter has provided a comprehensive understanding of how these environmental factors impact investment decisions and how investors can use this knowledge to make informed and responsible choices. In the next chapter, we will delve deeper into social considerations in ESG investing, including labor practices, community engagement, diversity, equity, inclusion, product safety, and consumer protection.

Chapter Summary

- Climate change and carbon emissions are major environmental challenges that pose significant risks to the global economy.
- Companies can reduce their carbon footprint by investing in renewable energy, implementing energy-efficient practices, and using clean technology.
- ESG investors are increasingly looking to invest in companies that are taking action to reduce their carbon footprint and mitigate the risks associated with climate change.
- Renewable energy and resource efficiency are important for achieving sustainable development.
- Biodiversity and habitat preservation are critical for maintaining the health and resilience of the planet's ecosystems.
- Companies must take action to protect and preserve biodiversity and habitats.
- Water management and pollution control are important considerations for ESG investing.
- Waste management and recycling programs help protect the environment and generate economic and social benefits for communities and businesses.

2

SOCIAL CONSIDERATIONS IN ESG INVESTING

This chapter delves into the crucial topic of evaluating and addressing social issues in ethical and sustainable investing. The chapter aims to provide readers with a comprehensive understanding of the various social considerations that should be considered when evaluating investments from an ESG perspective. The chapter will explore four key areas of social responsibility: labor and human rights, community engagement and development, diversity, equity, and inclusion, and product safety and consumer protection. By examining these topics, the chapter will provide readers with a framework for assessing and addressing social considerations in their investment decisions. Overall, this chapter will serve as a valuable resource for investors looking to incorporate social considerations into their ESG investing strategies.

Labor and Human Rights

ESG investing focuses on labor and human rights. Investors are looking for companies that treat their workers fairly and ethically, provide safe and healthy working conditions, and improve their supply chain. This can lead to long-term benefits for investors.

A weary factory worker stands amidst the chaos of machinery.

When companies are committed to labor and human rights, it can lead to many positive outcomes. It can also lead to a more socially responsible and ethical investment portfolio. This can be particularly important for those looking to align their investments with their values.

Moreover, companies with good labor and human rights record tend to have better employee retention, lower recruitment cost, and more loyal customers, which can lead to higher productivity, better financial performance, and sustainable growth. Therefore, ESG investing, which puts labor and human rights as critical components, can also help investors achieve their financial goals while doing good for society.

Overall, ESG investing is a way for investors to take a more holistic approach. By focusing on labor and human rights, they can promote fair treatment of workers, positively impact the local communities, contribute to a more sustainable global economy, and achieve their financial goals.

Community Engagement and Development

Community engagement and development are also important components of social considerations in ESG investing. This includes ensuring that a company is engaged with the communities in which it operates and is committed to promoting the development and well-being of these communities. Companies that do not engage with their communities and do not contribute to their development can face **significant** reputational, legal, and financial risks. Additionally, it can also lead to a negative impact on the company's ability to attract and retain employees and customers. Finally, it can also lead to a negative impact on the local communities where they operate.

ESG investors are increasingly looking to invest in companies committed to community engagement and development. This can include investing in companies that have strong community engagement policies and are committed to promoting the development and well-being of the communities in which they operate. This can include training and education programs, supporting local charities and community organizations, and investing in community development projects.

Additionally, investors can invest in companies committed to contributing to the development of local communities through philanthropy and other initiatives. This can include providing financial support to local charities, volunteering with local organizations, and supporting local entrepreneurs. Furthermore, companies committed to community engagement and development are more likely to positively impact the local communities where they operate, which can lead to long-term sustainability.

In conclusion, community engagement and development are important components of social considerations in ESG investing. Investing in companies committed to community engagement and development can promote the development and well-being of the communities in which they operate and contribute to the long-term sustainability of the company and the local community. This can lead to long-term financial benefits for investors and contribute to a more sustainable global economy.

A bustling farmer's market in a vibrant community where locals gather to shop for fresh produce and connect with their neighbors.

Diversity, Equity, and Inclusion

Diversity, equity, and inclusion have increasingly become focal points for socially conscious investors in environmental, social, and governance (ESG) investing. These considerations are crucial for ensuring that a company is committed to promoting and fostering a culture of diversity, equity, and inclusion in all aspects of its operations, from the workplace to its interactions with customers, suppliers, and other stakeholders.

Failing to promote and maintain a diverse and inclusive environment can have significant consequences for a company, including reputational risks, legal and financial repercussions, and potentially even a loss of customers or investors. As such, ESG investors are becoming more discerning and are looking to invest in companies that demonstrate a commitment to diversity, equity, and inclusion.

One way to do this is by investing in companies that have implemented strong policies and initiatives to promote diversity, equity, and inclusion in the workplace, including programs that support underrepresented groups and provide training and education on these issues. Additionally, investors can look for companies committed to promoting diversity, equity, and inclusion in their supply chains and the communities in which they operate, as well as those with a track record of supporting and partnering with organizations that advocate for diversity and inclusion.

In short, investing in companies that prioritize diversity, equity, and inclusion aligns with the values of socially conscious investors. Moreover, it mitigates potential reputational and financial risks for the company. As such, it is becoming an increasingly important consideration for ESG investors.

Product Safety and Consumer Protection

Environmental, social, and governance (ESG) investing is a rapidly growing field that focuses on the impact of a company's actions on the environment, society, and governance. One important aspect of ESG investing is evaluating a company's commitment to product safety and consumer protection.

Product safety refers to the measures a company takes to ensure that its products are free from defects and are not harmful to consumers. On the other hand, consumer protection refers to how a company ensures that consumers are not misled or taken advantage of in the marketplace.

When evaluating a company's commitment to product safety and consumer protection, investors should consider factors such as the company's history of product recalls, compliance with industry regulations, and transparency in disclosing product-related information to consumers.

One important consideration for investors is a company's history of product recalls. Companies with a history of recalling products due to safety concerns may be at a higher risk for future recalls, leading to financial losses and damaging the company's reputation.

Another important consideration is a company's compliance with industry regulations. Companies that are found to be non-compliant with industry regulations may be at a higher risk of facing penalties and fines, which can also lead to financial losses.

Investors should also consider a company's transparency in disclosing product-related information to consumers. Companies that are transparent in their product labeling and marketing practices are more likely to be trusted by consumers, which can lead to long-term financial success.

Overall, evaluating a company's commitment to product safety and consumer protection is an important aspect of ESG investing. Companies prioritizing these issues are more likely to be responsible corporate citizens and more likely to be **financially successful** in the long term.

In conclusion, this chapter has provided an in-depth examination of the social considerations that should be considered when evaluating investments from an ESG perspective. The chapter has explored labor and human rights, community engagement and development, diversity, equity, and inclusion, and product safety and consumer protection as key areas of social responsibility that investors should consider when making investment decisions. By understanding and addressing these social considerations, investors can make more informed decisions that align with their values and contribute to a more sustainable and just society.

As we have seen, social considerations are essential to ESG investing. However, they are not the only component. Governance considerations, such as a company's management structure and ethical practices, also play a crucial role in determining an investment's overall sustainability and ethicality. Therefore, the next chapter will delve into governance considerations in ESG investing and provide a framework for evaluating and addressing these considerations in your investment decisions. By understanding and addressing environmental, social, and governance considerations, investors can make ethical and sustainable investment decisions that align with their values and contribute to a more just and equitable society.

Chapter Summary

- ESG investing focuses on labor and human rights, community engagement and development, diversity, equity, inclusion, product safety, and consumer protection.
- Companies prioritizing labor and human rights tend to have better employee retention, lower recruitment costs, and more loyal customers.
- Companies committed to community engagement and development are more likely to positively impact the local communities where they operate.
- Diversity, equity, and inclusion are important social considerations in ESG investing.
- Product safety and consumer protection are important aspects of ESG investing.
- Companies with a history of product recall and non-compliance with industry regulations may be at a higher risk of facing financial losses.
- Companies that are transparent in their product labeling and marketing practices are more likely to be trusted by consumers.
- Understanding and addressing environmental, social, and governance considerations is essential for ethical and sustainable investment decisions.

3

GOVERNANCE CONSIDERATIONS IN ESG INVESTING

This chapter will explore the various governance considerations crucial in environmental, social, and governance (ESG) investing. The topics covered in this chapter include corporate governance and executive compensation, transparency and disclosure, political lobbying and advocacy, anti-corruption and bribery policies, and tax transparency and responsible tax practices. These topics are essential for understanding corporate governance's impact on a company's performance and sustainability and how it affects investment decision-making. This chapter aims to provide readers with a comprehensive understanding of the governance considerations central to ESG investing and how we can use them to evaluate potential investments. Overall, this chapter will provide readers with the knowledge and tools necessary to make informed investment decisions based on governance considerations within the ESG framework.

Corporate Governance and Executive Compensation

Corporate governance is vital to managing and operating a company effectively and efficiently. It refers to the set of rules, practices, and processes that are put in place to ensure that a company is properly directed and controlled. Good corporate governance is essential for creating an environment where a company can thrive and succeed.

Good corporate governance is important not only for a company's internal operations but also for external stakeholders. ESG investing is a growing trend in the investing world, and good corporate governance is **crucial** to this type of investing. ESG investors are looking at a company's financial performance and considering its impact on the environment, society, and the way it governs itself. A company with strong corporate governance is more likely to be well-managed, accountable, and responsive to the needs of its stakeholders. This can lead to better financial performance and greater stability over the long term, which is beneficial for both the company and its investors.

A close-up shot of a large ornate desk with a stack of papers a pen and a calculator sitting on top.

In addition to the financial benefits, good corporate governance also helps to promote ethical behavior and integrity within a company. It helps to ensure that a company is run with transparency, fairness, and accountability, which can foster trust and confidence among stakeholders. This can lead to a positive reputation for the company, which can be beneficial in attracting and retaining customers, employees, and investors.

Executive compensation is an important aspect of corporate governance that investors should carefully consider. The amount of compensation paid to executives can provide insight into the level of alignment between management and shareholders. High levels of executive compensation may be a sign that the interests of management are not aligned with the interests of shareholders and that the company is not being run in the best interests of its stakeholders.

Investors should look at executive compensation when evaluating a company and compare it to industry standards and peers. They should also consider the company's performance and whether the compensation levels are commensurate with its financial results. If executive compensation is high, it may signify a need for greater alignment between management and shareholders.

In addition to evaluating executive compensation levels, investors should also look for companies that have adopted governance practices that align the interests of management with those of shareholders. This can include practices such as providing shareholders with an advisory vote on executive compensation, having independent directors on the board, and implementing performance-based compensation. These practices ensure that the company's management maximizes value for all stakeholders rather than just themselves.

Overall, corporate governance is essential to a company's effective and efficient management. It involves a set of rules, practices, and processes that ensure a company is properly directed and controlled. Good corporate governance is important not only for a company's internal operations but also for external stakeholders. It is crucial for ESG investing, a growing trend in the investing world. Companies with strong corporate governance are more likely to be well-managed, accountable, and responsive to the needs of their stakeholders, leading to better financial performance and greater stability over the long term. Additionally, good corporate governance promotes ethical behavior and integrity within a company, fostering trust and confidence among stakeholders. Investors should carefully evaluate executive compensation levels and look for companies that have adopted governance practices that align the interests of management with those of shareholders.

Transparency and Disclosure

Transparency and disclosure are critical elements in ensuring proper corporate governance. These concepts are paramount for investors, as they clearly understand a company's operations, financial performance, and potential risks. In addition, this level of transparency and disclosure allows investors to make informed decisions based on accurate and up-to-date information and helps to build trust between a company and its investors.

Companies that demonstrate a strong commitment to transparency and disclosure are generally considered to be better governed than those that do not. This is because **transparency and disclosure are key indicators** of a company's commitment to ethical and responsible business practices. In addition, by providing investors with detailed information about the company's operations and performance, companies can demonstrate their commitment to being accountable for their actions.

Moreover, transparency and disclosure also play a vital role in building trust between a company and its stakeholders. When companies are open and transparent in communicating with investors, they are more likely to be viewed as trustworthy and responsible corporate citizens. This, in turn, can improve the company's overall reputation and enhance its standing in the business community.

Overall, transparency and disclosure are essential components of good corporate governance. By providing investors with accurate and up-to-date information about the company's operations and performance, companies can demonstrate their commitment to ethical and responsible business practices and help to build trust between the company and its investors. This ultimately leads to a more responsible and sustainable corporate culture, which benefits all stakeholders.

Political Lobbying and Advocacy

Regarding governance considerations, political lobbying and advocacy play a crucial role. Companies that engage in these activities have the potential to shape public policy and regulations significantly. This is why it is essential for investors to be aware of a company's lobbying and advocacy efforts and to evaluate whether they align with their values and investment goals.

Lobbying is the act of attempting to influence decisions made by government officials, primarily legislators and members of regulatory agencies. Businesses can do this through direct communication with legislators, grassroots campaigns to mobilize public support, or funding third-party organizations that advocate for specific policies. Conversely, advocacy is publicly supporting or opposing a particular issue or policy.

Companies engage in lobbying and advocacy for various reasons. For example, they may seek to influence regulations that directly affect their business, such as environmental laws or taxes. They may also seek to shape broader policy issues that indirectly impact their operations, such as healthcare or trade policy.

While lobbying and advocacy can benefit companies, they can also have negative consequences. For example, a company that lobbies for policies that harm the environment or undermine workers' rights may be seen as unethical by some investors. Additionally, a company that spends significant money on lobbying may be viewed as diverting resources away from more productive uses.

In light of these considerations, investors should be aware of a company's lobbying and advocacy activities and assess whether they align with their values and investment goals. Investors can do this by researching a company's lobbying spending and agenda and looking into the company's public statements and advocacy efforts. By taking these steps, investors can make more informed decisions about the companies they invest in.

Anti-Corruption and Bribery Policies

Anti-corruption and bribery policies are essential elements of good governance. They are increasingly being recognized as important considerations in responsible and sustainable investing. This section will explore the risks and opportunities associated with corruption and bribery in environmental, social, and governance (ESG) investing.

First, it is important to understand the scope of the problem. Corruption and bribery are pervasive issues affecting virtually every sector and region worldwide. According to the World Bank, corruption costs the global economy **$2 trillion annually.** In addition to financial costs, corruption and bribery undermine the rule of law, erode trust in institutions, and lead to human rights violations.

For investors, the risks associated with corruption and bribery include reputational damage, legal and regulatory enforcement actions, and reduced financial performance. For example, companies that engage in corrupt or bribery practices may be subject to fines, penalties, and legal action, leading to significant financial losses for investors. In addition, companies that are known to be involved in corruption or bribery may find it more difficult to access capital markets and may face increased scrutiny from regulators, rating agencies, and other stakeholders.

However, there are also opportunities for investors who take a proactive approach to address corruption and bribery risks in their portfolios. For example, many companies have implemented anti-corruption and anti-bribery policies and procedures to mitigate these risks. As a result, these companies may be better positioned to navigate the legal and regulatory landscape. As a result, they may be more attractive to investors looking for companies that prioritize good governance.

ESG investors can take several steps to identify and mitigate corruption and bribery risks in their portfolios. These include:

- Incorporating anti-corruption and anti-bribery considerations into investment analysis and decision-making processes.
- Engaging with companies to understand their policies and practices related to corruption and bribery and encouraging them to adopt best practices in this area.
- Collaborating with other investors and stakeholders to promote transparency and accountability in the companies they invest in.
- Monitoring and reporting on companies' performance regarding anti-corruption and anti-bribery policies and practices.

In conclusion, anti-corruption and anti-bribery policies are essential elements of good governance and responsible investing. Investors should be aware of the risks associated with corruption and bribery and take steps to identify and mitigate them in their portfolios. By promoting transparency, accountability, and good governance, ESG investors can help to create a more sustainable and responsible global economy.

Tax Transparency and Responsible Tax Practices

As environmental, social, and governance (ESG) investing grows, responsible tax practices are increasingly important focus areas for investors and companies. This includes compliance with local and international tax laws and transparency and fairness in how taxes are paid and reported.

One key aspect of tax transparency is the ability of investors to understand a company's tax footprint. This includes information on where and how much the company is paying in taxes and any potential tax avoidance or evasion practices. Unfortunately, this information can be difficult to obtain, as many companies keep this information private. However, investors can use several resources, such as the Tax Justice

Network's Financial Secrecy Index, to better understand a company's tax practices.

Another important aspect of responsible tax practices is the concept of *"fair tax."* This refers to the idea that companies should pay their fair share of taxes in the countries where they operate and earn profits. This can include measures such as avoiding tax havens, paying taxes at a rate commensurate with the company's level of profits, and avoiding aggressive tax planning strategies.

In addition to the above, responsible tax practices also include compliance with local and international tax laws and not engaging in any illegal activities related to taxes. Many companies today have tax policies that ensure compliance with all laws and regulations, which is important for protecting the company and its investors.

An open book on a wooden desk with a pen resting on top beside it a calculator and a stack of papers.

As investors increasingly focus on ESG factors, companies need to be transparent and responsible in their tax practices. This can build trust with investors and contribute to long-term financial success.

Overall, tax transparency and responsible tax practices are important aspects of ESG investing. Investors can use resources to understand a company's tax practices better. Companies should be transparent and responsible in their tax practices to build trust with investors and contribute to long-term success.

In conclusion, this chapter has examined the various governance considerations crucial in environmental, social, and governance (ESG) investing. We have explored corporate governance and executive compensation, transparency and disclosure, political lobbying and advocacy, anti-corruption and bribery policies, and tax transparency and responsible tax practices. These topics are essential for understanding corporate governance's impact on a company's performance and sustainability and how it affects investment decision-making. The information presented in this chapter has highlighted the importance of considering governance considerations as a fundamental aspect of the ESG investment process. Understanding and evaluating these considerations allows investors to make more informed and responsible investment decisions.

With the knowledge gained in this chapter, readers are now equipped to move on to the next chapter, *"Integrating ESG Considerations into Investment Strategy."* This next chapter will build on the information presented in this book by providing practical examples and strategies for incorporating ESG considerations into an overall investment strategy.

Chapter Summary

- Corporate governance is essential to a company's effective and efficient management and is important for ESG investing.

- Good corporate governance promotes ethical behavior and integrity within a company, fostering trust and confidence among stakeholders.
- Transparency and disclosure are essential components of good corporate governance, allowing investors to make informed decisions based on accurate and up-to-date information.
- Political lobbying and advocacy can benefit companies but can also have negative consequences if they do not align with investors' values and investment goals.
- Anti-corruption and bribery policies are essential elements of good governance and responsible investing.
- Investors should be aware of a company's lobbying and advocacy activities and assess whether they align with their values and investment goals.
- Tax transparency and responsible tax practices are important aspects of ESG investing.
- Understanding and evaluating governance considerations allows investors to make more informed and responsible investment decisions.

4

INTEGRATING ESG CONSIDERATIONS INTO INVESTMENT STRATEGY

Environmental, social, and governance (ESG) considerations are increasingly important in the investment world. As more investors recognize the potential risks and opportunities associated with these issues, many are looking for ways to integrate ESG considerations into their investment strategies. This chapter will explore three key approaches to integrating ESG considerations into investment strategy: screening and exclusion, active ownership and engagement, and impact investing.

Screening and Exclusion

Screening and exclusion is a well-established method for integrating environmental, social, and governance (ESG) considerations into investment strategies. The process involves identifying companies or sectors that do not meet specific ESG criteria and subsequently excluding them from an investment portfolio. This approach is particularly useful for investors seeking to minimize potential risks associated with ESG issues while aligning their investments with their values.

One of the key aspects of screening and exclusion is identifying companies or sectors that do not meet the ESG criteria. Investors can do this through various methods, such as publicly available data on environmental performance, social impact, or governance practices or by engaging third-party ESG rating agencies. Once the companies or sectors that do not meet the ESG criteria have been identified, they can be excluded from the portfolio. This helps to ensure that the portfolio is composed of companies aligned with the investor's values and goals.

For example, investors may exclude companies with poor environmental records, such as those identified as major polluters or involved in environmental controversies. Similarly, investors may exclude companies involved in controversial business practices, such as those associated with human rights abuses or corruption. By excluding these companies, investors can **minimize the potential risks** associated with these issues and align their investments with their values.

In addition to minimizing potential risks, screening and exclusion can help investors capitalize on opportunities associated with ESG issues. For instance, by excluding companies with poor environmental records, an investor may be able to invest in companies that are leaders in sustainable practices, potentially leading to better long-term financial performance. Similarly, by excluding companies with poor governance practices, an investor may be able to invest in companies with strong corporate governance structures, potentially leading to better financial performance.

In conclusion, screening and exclusion is a well-established method for integrating ESG considerations into investment strategies. By identifying and excluding companies or sectors that do not meet specific ESG criteria, investors can minimize potential risks associated with ESG issues, align their investments with their values and capitalize on opportunities associated with ESG issues. Moreover, as the awareness and importance of ESG issues continue to grow, more investors will likely adopt this approach to integrate ESG considerations into their investment strategies.

Active Ownership and Engagement

Active ownership and engagement is a powerful strategy for integrating environmental, social, and governance (ESG) considerations into investment decisions. This approach involves actively engaging with companies where an investor holds shares and encouraging them to improve their performance in areas related to ESG.

One key aspect of active ownership is using voting rights as shareholders to support or oppose resolutions related to ESG issues. For example, an investor may vote in favor of a resolution to reduce a company's carbon emissions or against a resolution that would weaken labor protections for workers. By using their voting rights in this way, investors can help to promote positive change within companies and encourage them to prioritize ESG considerations.

A group of young business-people huddled around a bustling street-side café.

Another important aspect of active ownership is direct engagement with company management. Investors can use this opportunity to discuss specific ESG issues with company leaders and encourage them to take action to improve their performance in these areas. For example, this might involve discussing reducing a company's environmental impact, improving labor practices, or increasing transparency and accountability. Through these engagements, investors can help to build a more sustainable and responsible corporate sector.

In addition to promoting positive change within companies, active ownership and engagement can also help enhance investors' long-term returns. By encouraging companies to prioritize ESG considerations, investors can help to build more sustainable and resilient businesses that are better positioned to navigate the challenges of the 21st century. This can ultimately lead to better financial outcomes for investors over the long term.

Overall, active ownership and engagement is a valuable approach for integrating ESG considerations into investment strategy and one that can help to promote positive change within companies and enhance long-term returns for investors.

Impact Investing

A third approach to integrating ESG considerations into investment strategy is "*impact investing.*" This investment strategy involves directing capital toward companies, projects, or funds with a positive social or environmental impact. This approach to investing is based on the idea that financial returns and positive impact can go hand in hand. Investing in companies working towards solutions to pressing social and environmental issues, investors can achieve a financial return and contribute to creating a more sustainable and equitable world.

For example, an impact investor may choose to invest in a renewable energy company working to reduce greenhouse gas emissions or a company that provides affordable housing to low-income communities. These types of investments not only have the potential to generate financial returns but also provide a tangible positive impact on the world.

In addition to providing a way for investors to align their investments with their values, impact investing can offer several other benefits. For example, investments in sustainable and responsible companies may be less risky in the long term, as they are less likely to be impacted by negative social or environmental events. Impact investing can also help create jobs and economic opportunities in underserved communities.

Overall, impact investing is a powerful approach to integrating ESG considerations into an investment strategy. By investing in companies, projects, or funds with a positive social or environmental impact, investors can achieve a double bottom line of financial return and positive impact.

In conclusion, integrating ESG considerations into investment strategy is important for investors to manage potential risks and capitalize on opportunities associated with these issues. The approaches described in this chapter, including screening and exclusion, active ownership and engagement, and impact investing, can help investors to align their investments with their values and promote positive change in the world. As the awareness and importance of ESG issues continue to grow, more investors will likely adopt these and other approaches to integrate ESG considerations into their investment strategies.

Chapter Summary

- Screening and exclusion is a well-established method for integrating ESG considerations into investment strategies, involving identifying and excluding companies or sectors that do not meet specific ESG criteria.
- Active ownership and engagement involve actively engaging with companies where an investor holds shares and encouraging them to improve their performance in areas related to ESG.

- Impact investing involves directing capital toward companies, projects, or funds with a positive social or environmental impact.
- Screening and exclusion can help investors minimize potential risks associated with ESG issues and align their investments with their values.
- Active ownership and engagement can help to promote positive change within companies and enhance long-term returns for investors.
- Impact investing can provide a way for investors to align their investments with their values and achieve a double bottom line of financial return and positive impact.
- Integrating ESG considerations into investment strategy is important for investors to manage potential risks and capitalize on opportunities associated with these issues.
- As the awareness and importance of ESG issues continue to grow, more investors will likely adopt these approaches to integrate ESG considerations into their investment strategies.

5

MEASURING AND EVALUATING ESG PERFORMANCE

Measuring and evaluating the performance of environmental, social, and governance (ESG) factors is a crucial aspect of responsible investing. In this chapter, we will discuss the various methods of assessing ESG performance, including using ratings and indices and analyzing company-specific data. We will also address the limitations and challenges of ESG measurement.

ESG Ratings and Indices

ESG, or environmental, social, and governance, is a term used to describe the three central factors that investors and analysts consider when evaluating a company's overall performance and potential for growth. One of the most widely accepted and recognized methods for measuring and evaluating a company's ESG performance is through the use of ratings and indices provided by third-party organizations.

These organizations, such as Sustainalytics, MSCI, and FTSE Russell, assess companies based on predefined criteria focusing on environmental impact, human rights, and corporate governance. These criteria are designed to provide a comprehensive and unbiased evaluation of a company's overall performance and potential for growth.

MSCI ESG rating system demonstrating what it takes to become a laggard, average, or leader business. Source: MSCI

Once a company has been assessed, it is given a rating or score that can be used to compare its performance to that of its peers. This allows investors and analysts to quickly and easily identify companies performing well in ESG and make more informed decisions about where to invest their money. Additionally, these ratings and indices can also be used by companies themselves to identify areas where they need to improve and to set goals for future performance.

Overall, ESG ratings and indices are valuable tools for investors, analysts, and companies, providing a clear and concise way to evaluate a company's performance and potential for growth in the long term. It is also an important tool for society to ensure sustainable development of society. Using ESG ratings and indices is becoming increasingly popular among investors and companies as they recognize the importance of considering ESG factors when making investment decisions. It helps promote sustainable and responsible business practices, which ultimately benefit society and the environment.

Assessing Company-Specific ESG Data

Assessing company-specific environmental, social, and governance (ESG) data is crucial for measuring and evaluating a company's performance in these areas. This analysis includes an in-depth examination of various aspects of a company's operations, such as its carbon emissions, labor practices, and political lobbying. This information can be obtained from various sources, including a company's annual reports, sustainability reports, and other publicly available documents.

By analyzing this data, investors can gain a more detailed understanding of a company's ESG performance and identify areas for improvement. For example, an investor may find that a company has a high level of carbon emissions and decide to invest in a company with lower emissions. Similarly, an investor may find a company with poor labor practices and choose to invest in a company with better labor standards.

Furthermore, by assessing company-specific ESG data, investors can also compare the performance of different companies in the same industry. This can provide valuable insights into the industry's overall performance in terms of ESG and help investors make more informed investment decisions.

Additionally, assessing company-specific ESG data can help investors identify companies that are leaders in the field. These companies may be more likely to be successful in the long term as they are more likely to be responsive to the growing demand for sustainable and socially responsible investments.

In summary, assessing company-specific ESG data is essential for measuring and evaluating a company's performance in these areas. It allows investors to gain a more detailed understanding of a company's ESG performance, identify areas for improvement, compare the performance of different companies in the same industry and identify companies that are leaders in the field. This can assist investors in making more informed investment decisions.

The Limitations and Challenges of ESG Measurement

The increasing use of environmental, social, and governance (ESG) measurements to assess companies' sustainability and ethical performance has brought several limitations and challenges to light. One of the most significant limitations is the need for more **standardized**

reporting and criteria to evaluate ESG performance. This can make it challenging to compare the ESG performance of different companies, as there needs to be a clear, consistent framework for measurement.

A team of scientists huddled around a large computer screen eagerly analyzing data and discussing their findings.

Furthermore, there needs to be more transparency and reliability in the data that companies report, which can make it difficult to assess performance accurately. This is partly because there is no uniform method for collecting and reporting ESG data, which can lead to inconsistent or incomplete information. Additionally, Bad actors may incentivize companies to present their performance in the most favorable light, which can lead to biased or misleading data.

Another limitation is the need for more objective and comparable data in certain ESG areas, such as human rights or social factors, which can make it difficult to evaluate the performance of companies in these areas. Furthermore, the need for more consensus on what constitutes good performance in certain ESG areas, such as climate change or labor rights, can make it difficult to establish clear standards for measurement.

Overall, while the use of ESG measurement has grown in popularity, it is important to acknowledge these limitations and challenges to improve the accuracy and reliability of ESG assessments. Businesses can achieve this through more standardized reporting and criteria, increased data transparency and reliability, and addressing the need for more objective and comparable data in certain ESG areas.

In conclusion, measuring and evaluating ESG performance is important for responsible investing. But, there are limitations and challenges, such as the need for standardization and transparency. Despite these challenges, assessing ESG performance is crucial for making informed investment decisions and promoting sustainable business practices.

Chapter Summary

- Measuring and evaluating environmental, social, and governance (ESG) performance is an important aspect of responsible investing.
- Ratings and indices provided by third-party organizations are widely accepted and recognized methods for assessing ESG performance.
- Companies can use these ratings and indices to identify areas for improvement and set goals for future performance.
- Assessing company-specific ESG data is also important for measuring and evaluating a company's performance in these areas.
- This data can be used to compare the performance of different companies in the same industry and identify companies that are leaders in the field.
- There are several limitations and challenges to ESG measurement, such as the need for more standardized reporting and criteria, increased data transparency and reliability, and more objective and comparable data in certain ESG areas.

- Despite these challenges, assessing ESG performance is important in making informed investment decisions and promoting sustainable business practices.
- Companies can address these challenges by implementing more standardized reporting and criteria, increasing data transparency and reliability, and addressing the need for more objective and comparable data in certain ESG areas.

6

THE ROLE OF REGULATORS AND GOVERNMENT IN ESG INVESTING

As the world becomes increasingly focused on environmental, social, and governance (ESG) issues, the role of regulators and government in ESG investing is becoming more important. As a result, ESG investing, which involves investing in companies that prioritize these issues, is gaining popularity as investors seek to align their values with their investments. However, the regulatory framework for ESG investing is still evolving, and government policies and initiatives significantly shape the industry. In this chapter, we will explore the regulatory framework for ESG investing, government policies and initiatives promoting ESG investing, and the influence of global regulatory developments on ESG investing.

The Regulatory Framework for ESG Investing

As environmental, social, and governance (ESG) investing continues to expand, the regulatory framework surrounding it is also evolving to keep pace. While there may not be a universally accepted definition of ESG investing, it is clear that the principles and guidelines developed by regulators in various countries are becoming increasingly crucial.

In the European Union, for example, the European Commission has been working to promote sustainable finance through various initiatives and regulations, including the Taxonomy Regulation, which provides a framework for classifying environmentally sustainable economic activities. Similarly, in the United States, the SEC has issued guidance on how companies can disclose their ESG risks and opportunities.

These guidelines and regulations are important for ensuring the **transparency and reliability** of ESG investing for investors and promoting consistency across the industry. In addition, they help to ensure that companies are held accountable for their ESG performance and that investors can make informed decisions about where to allocate their capital.

It is, therefore, important for market participants to stay informed about the regulatory developments in the ESG investing space, as it is likely to continue to shape the industry in the future.

Government Policies and Initiatives Promoting ESG Investing

Governments worldwide increasingly recognize the importance of promoting environmentally and socially responsible investing, also known as ESG investing. In addition to creating a regulatory framework that supports ESG investing, governments are also implementing various policies and initiatives to encourage this investing. These policies can take many forms, such as tax incentives, grants, and subsidies.

One example of a government promoting ESG investing is the United Kingdom. The UK government has introduced several measures to encourage ESG investing, including creating the Green Investment Bank. This institution is designed to fund projects that promote environmental sustainability, such as renewable energy and low-carbon transportation. The UK government has also established the Green Bonds Market, which allows companies and organizations to issue bonds specifically earmarked for environmental projects.

Similarly, in the United States, the government has also taken steps to promote ESG investing. One example of this is the establishment of the Green Bank, which provides funding for clean energy projects. The US also has a Green Bond Market, which works similarly to the UK Green Bonds Market.

Overall, government policies and initiatives play an important role in promoting ESG investing by creating a supportive environment for these investments. Investors need to be aware of the different incentives and programs available to them, as these can make a significant difference in the long-term financial performance of their investments.

A stern-faced government official.

The Influence of Global Regulatory Developments on ESG Investing

The impact of global regulatory developments on environmental, social, and governance (ESG) investing is of increasing importance as the popularity and growth of ESG investing continue to rise. The proliferation of ESG investing, which focuses on investing in companies that positively impact environmental and social issues, in addition to traditional financial considerations, has led to a growing need for clear and consistent guidelines and standards for responsible investing.

In response to this need, various international organizations and governing bodies have developed principles and guidelines for responsible investing. One notable example is the United Nations, which has established the Principles for Responsible Investment (PRI), a set of six principles that provide a framework for responsible investing and promote the integration of ESG considerations into investment decision-making. The PRI aims to encourage the adoption of responsible investing practices worldwide and has been adopted by many investors and investment managers.

Another important global regulatory development in sustainable finance is the Financial Stability Board's (FSB) Task Force on Climate-related Financial Disclosures (TCFD). The TCFD has developed a set of recommendations for the disclosure of climate-related financial information, which guides companies on disclosing the potential financial impacts of climate-related risks and opportunities in their financial filings. The TCFD's recommendations are designed to **promote transparency and consistency** in the disclosure of climate-related financial information and are expected to play a key role in helping investors and other stakeholders to understand better and manage the financial risks and opportunities associated with climate change.

In addition to the PRI and TCFD, various other global regulatory developments are shaping the ESG investing industry. For example, the European Union has implemented regulations that require companies to disclose their non-financial information, including their ESG performance, in their annual reports. The Securities and Exchange Commission (SEC) in the United States has also issued guidance on disclosing ESG information by public companies. In addition, various countries and regions have also implemented their guidelines and regulations for responsible investing.

Overall, global regulatory developments significantly shape the ESG investing industry and influence how ESG considerations are integrated into investment decision-making. These developments will continue to shape the industry in the future. Investors and other stakeholders must stay informed about the latest regulatory developments and their implications for the ESG investing industry.

In conclusion, the role of regulators and government in ESG investing is becoming increasingly important as the industry grows. The regulatory framework for ESG investing is still evolving, but it is becoming increasingly important as the industry grows. Government policies and initiatives play an important role in promoting ESG investing, and global regulatory developments also significantly influence the industry. As ESG investing continues to grow in popularity, the regulatory framework and government policies will likely continue to evolve to meet the needs of investors and the industry.

Chapter Summary

- The role of regulators and government in ESG investing is becoming increasingly important.
- A regulatory framework for ESG investing is evolving, with guidelines and regulations from the European Commission and the SEC in the US.
- Governments are implementing various policies and initiatives to encourage ESG investing, such as tax incentives, grants, and subsidies.
- The UN has established the Principles for Responsible Investment (PRI) to provide a framework for responsible investing.
- The Financial Stability Board's (FSB) Task Force on Climate-related Financial Disclosures (TCFD) has developed a set of recommendations for the disclosure of climate-related financial information.
- The European Union has implemented regulations that require companies to disclose their non-financial

information, including their ESG performance, in their annual reports.

- The SEC in the US has issued guidance on disclosing ESG information by public companies.
- Global regulatory developments significantly shape the ESG investing industry and will continue to do so in the future.

7

ESG INVESTING AND FINANCIAL PERFORMANCE

ESG investing, which stands for environmental, social, and governance investing, is a rapidly growing field that has gained significant attention in recent years. ESG investing involves investing in companies with strong environmental, social, and governance practices. This chapter will examine the historical and current research on the relationship between ESG and financial performance, the potential risks and benefits of ESG investing for investors, and the role of active management in ESG investing.

The Historical and Current Research on the Relationship Between ESG and Financial Performance

The study of environmental, social, and governance (ESG) factors and financial performance has been a topic of interest for many years. Historically, there has been a diverse body of evidence regarding the correlation between ESG and financial performance. However, in recent years, many studies have revealed a **positive relationship** between companies prioritizing ESG factors and their financial performance.

A study conducted by the Morgan Stanley Institute for Sustainable

Investing found that companies with strong environmental, social, and governance (ESG) practices tend to have higher returns and lower volatility than their peers. Companies that prioritize ESG factors may be better equipped to identify and manage potential risks and capitalize on opportunities. Furthermore, these companies are more likely to have sound management, which is an important factor in achieving long-term financial performance. The study highlights that ESG practices are not just a matter of corporate responsibility. Still, they also directly impact a company's bottom line. Companies prioritizing ESG factors are more likely to have a sustainable business model, which is crucial in today's business environment. Investing in companies that have strong ESG practices can be a smart financial decision, as they are more likely to be resilient in the face of economic challenges and are better positioned to capitalize on growth opportunities in the long run.

Another study conducted by the Harvard Business Review found that companies with strong ESG practices tend to have better employee engagement and retention. This is because employees felt more connected to and invested in a company that positively impacted the world. Additionally, these companies tend to have a stronger brand and reputation, which can lead to increased customer loyalty and better business performance.

Furthermore, companies that prioritize ESG factors are more likely to be viewed as leaders in their industry, and this perception can lead to increased market share and revenue growth. This is because consumers are becoming increasingly conscious of the impact of their purchasing decisions on the environment and society, and they are more likely to support companies that align with their values.

The studies suggest that investing in companies with strong ESG practices is more than a socially responsible decision. Still, it can also be a financially savvy one. These companies are better equipped to manage risks, capitalize on opportunities, and achieve long-term financial performance. They also tend to have engaged employees, a strong brand, and a reputation for leadership in their industry, all of which contribute to their overall success.

This research supports the idea that incorporating ESG factors into investment decisions can improve long-term financial outcomes. It also highlights the importance of considering ESG factors as a potential indicator of a company's overall health and future potential. As more and more investors and organizations begin to recognize the importance of ESG factors in driving financial performance, incorporating ESG considerations into investment decisions will likely continue to gain traction.

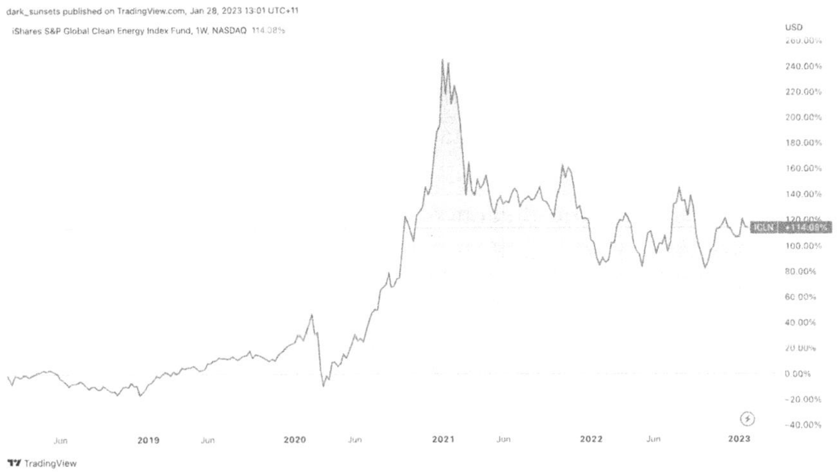

iShares S&P Global Clean Energy Index Fund 5 year chart showing a +114% return. Source: TradingView

The Potential Risks and Benefits of ESG Investing for Investors

Regarding ESG investing, it's important to consider both the potential risks and benefits for investors. ESG investing has gained significant attention in recent years as more and more investors are becoming aware of the impact that their investments can have on the world.

On the one hand, investing in companies that prioritize and adhere to strong ESG practices can lead to higher returns and lower volatility. This is because companies prioritizing sustainability tend to be more resilient and better able to navigate economic challenges, which can lead to more stable returns for investors. Additionally, companies with strong ESG practices may be more attractive to consumers and employees, leading to long-term growth and success.

However, companies may also need to be **more transparent** about their ESG practices. This could lead to investing in companies that are not truly sustainable or only paying lip service to the concept of sustainability without actually implementing meaningful change. Furthermore, some investors may be concerned that ESG investing may lead to lower returns than traditional investing, as companies may have to divert resources toward sustainability initiatives rather than growth and expansion.

In conclusion, while ESG investing presents potential risks and benefits for investors, it's important to consider both sides of the equation when making investment decisions. Investors should conduct thorough research and due diligence to invest in sustainable companies committed to positively impacting the world.

The Role of Active Management in ESG Investing

The importance of active management in environmental, social, and governance (ESG) investing cannot be overstated. Active managers take on the task of thoroughly researching and handpicking companies with a demonstrated commitment to strong ESG practices. This process involves evaluating a wide range of criteria, such as a company's environmental impact, treatment of employees, and governance structure, to ensure that they align with the values and principles of ESG investing.

In addition to the initial selection process, active managers also play a vital role in monitoring and engaging with the companies in which they have invested. This **ongoing engagement is crucial** as it allows them to stay informed about changes in a company's ESG practices and act accordingly. For example, suppose a company previously considered a leader in sustainable practices were to decrease its efforts in this area suddenly. In that case, active managers could detect this shift and decide whether to continue investing in the company.

Furthermore, active management can help investors ensure that the companies they invest in are committed to sustainability and not just paying lip service to the ESG movement. With active management, investors can have greater confidence that their money is being directed toward companies truly working to impact the world positively.

Ultimately, active management plays a crucial role in the ESG investing process. Through thorough research, ongoing monitoring, and engagement, active managers can identify and invest in companies that are truly committed to sustainable practices, providing investors with peace of mind that their money is being directed toward companies that align with their values.

In conclusion, ESG investing is a rapidly growing field that has recently gained significant attention. The research on the relationship between ESG and financial performance has found evidence of a positive relationship between the two. However, there are potential risks and benefits to ESG investing that investors should be aware of. Active management plays a crucial role in ESG investing by researching and selecting companies with strong ESG practices and monitoring and engaging with the companies in which they invest to ensure that they continue to meet the ESG criteria.

Chapter Summary

- ESG investing involves investing in companies with strong environmental, social, and governance practices.
- Studies have revealed a positive relationship between companies prioritizing ESG factors and their financial performance.
- Investing in companies that prioritize and adhere to strong ESG practices can lead to higher returns and lower volatility.

- ESG investing presents potential risks and benefits for investors. Therefore, when making investment decisions, it is important to consider both sides of the equation.
- Active management plays a crucial role in ESG investing by researching and selecting companies with strong ESG practices and monitoring and engaging with the companies in which they invest.
- Active management can help investors ensure that the companies they invest in are committed to sustainability and not just paying lip service to the ESG movement.
- Through thorough research, ongoing monitoring, and engagement, active managers can identify and invest in companies that are truly committed to sustainable practices.
- Investors should conduct thorough research and due diligence to invest in sustainable companies committed to positively impacting the world.

8

ESG INVESTING IN PRACTICE

Environmental, social, and governance (ESG) investing is a rapidly growing field, with more and more investors recognizing the benefits of incorporating these considerations into their investment strategies. However, the concept of ESG investing can be complex and difficult to implement in practice. This chapter will explore the practical aspects of ESG investing, including case studies of successful ESG investing strategies, best practices for implementing ESG investing in different asset classes and investment styles, and the role of investors, asset managers, and other stakeholders in advancing ESG investing.

Case Studies of Successful ESG Investing Strategies

The importance of environmental, social, and governance (ESG) investing has grown significantly in recent years as more and more investors recognize the potential benefits of investing in companies that prioritize sustainable practices and ethical governance. One of the best ways to understand the practical aspects of ESG investing is to look at real-world examples of successful strategies. In this section, we will explore three case studies of successful ESG investing strategies that have demonstrated the financial potential of investing in companies with strong ESG practices.

Case Study 1: Calvert Research and Management

Calvert Research and Management is a highly respected, well-established sustainable, responsible investment solutions provider. With over 40 years of experience in the industry, they have developed a reputation for excellence in ESG-integrated portfolio management.

At the core of Calvert's investment philosophy is a deep commitment to environmental sustainability, social responsibility, and corporate governance. As a result, they take a comprehensive and holistic approach to evaluating companies' performance, carefully analyzing their environmental practices and governance structures to identify firms that are best positioned to create long-term value for all stakeholders.

To achieve this goal, Calvert employs a rigorous research and analysis process incorporating a wide range of data and metrics. For example, they carefully review companies' environmental performance, assessing their energy usage, carbon emissions, water management, and other critical factors. They also evaluate companies' governance practices, looking at factors such as board composition, executive compensation, and transparency.

Through this process, Calvert can identify those companies that are truly committed to sustainable and responsible business practices. They then use this information to create tailored portfolios to meet their client's specific needs and goals. Whether through impact investing, ESG integration, or sustainable portfolio construction, Calvert's goal is to help investors achieve their financial objectives while positively impacting the world.

Calvert Research and Management has a proven track record of delivering outstanding performance with its ESG-integrated portfolios. One of the key indicators of this success is the consistent outperformance of their portfolios compared to their benchmarks. For example, over the last decade, ending December 2022, the Calvert Environmental Solutions Fund has demonstrated exceptional returns, delivering an annualized return of 14.26%. This performance compares favorably to the Russell 1000 Growth Index benchmark, which returned 14.09% annualized over the same period.

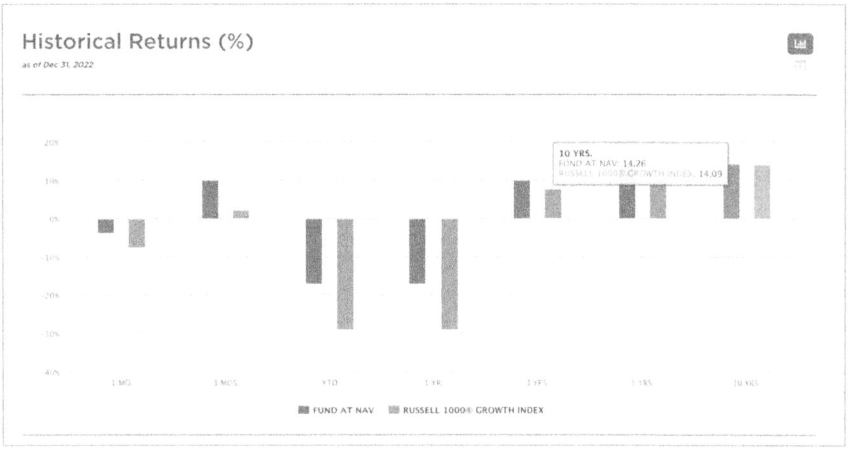

A series of bar charts highlighting Calvert Research and Management's positive historical returns over ten years. Source: Calvert Research and Management

This consistent outperformance is a testament to Calvert's expertise and commitment to integrating environmental, social, and governance (ESG) factors into the investment process. By carefully researching and analyzing companies' environmental performance and governance practices, Calvert can identify those well-positioned firms to create long-term value for stakeholders. By including these companies in their portfolios, Calvert can generate returns that are competitive with traditional investments while positively impacting the world.

Furthermore, Calvert's approach to ESG integration is not limited to a single investment strategy or fund. Instead, Calvert's expertise in ESG integration can be found across their entire product line, from impact investing to sustainable portfolio construction, allowing investors to align their investment goals with their values.

In conclusion, Calvert Research and Management has a long history of delivering strong performance with its ESG-integrated portfolios. The consistent outperformance of the Calvert Environmental

Solutions Fund compared to its benchmark is just one example of the company's ability to deliver strong returns while positively impacting the world. Investors looking to align their financial goals with their values can be confident that Calvert's expertise in ESG integration will help them achieve their objectives.

Case Study 2: Impax Asset Management

Impax Asset Management is a highly respected and accomplished global investment manager focusing on investing in companies actively working towards building a more sustainable economy. Their approach to investing is grounded in a comprehensive examination of a company's environmental, social, and governance (ESG) performance.

To ensure that they are making informed investment decisions, Impax has developed a proprietary rating system that allows them to evaluate companies on a wide range of ESG factors. These factors include but are not limited to, a company's carbon emissions, water usage, and labor practices. This system enables Impax to identify companies that are truly committed to sustainability and are making meaningful progress in this area. By investing in these companies, Impax can generate strong returns for its clients and contribute to the transition to a more sustainable economy.

Impax Asset Management has consistently demonstrated that its approach to investing, which integrates environmental, social, and governance (ESG) considerations, can generate strong returns for its clients. With £35 billion of assets under management, they generated £72.6 million profit before tax in the year ending 2021. However, the true value of Impax's approach to investing goes beyond financial returns. The company's commitment to ESG investing practices has had a tangible positive impact on the world around us. Impax is helping to drive the transition to a more sustainable economy by carefully selecting companies with a strong track record of responsible environmental and social practices. Additionally, by engaging with companies on ESG issues and encouraging them to improve their practices, Impax is helping to create a more responsible business environment.

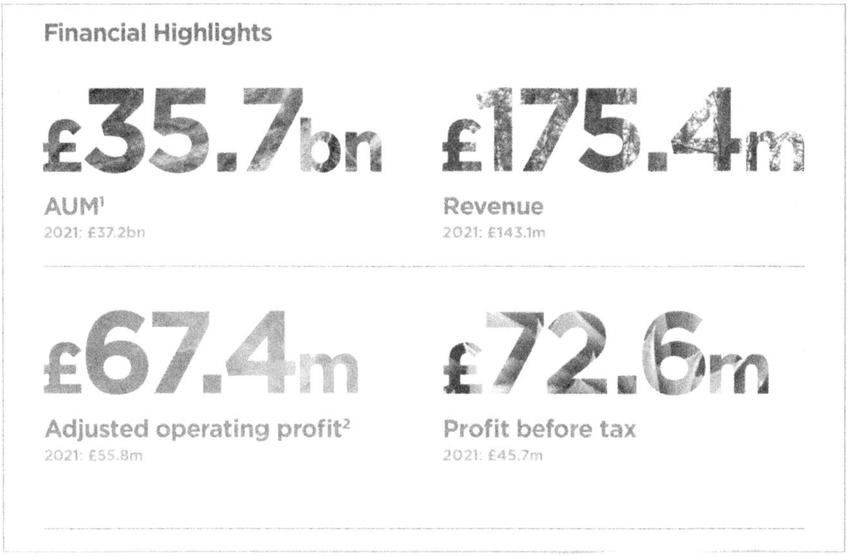

A figure describing Impax Asset Management's positive financial highlights from 2021. Source: Impax Asset Management

In conclusion, Impax's ESG-integrated approach to investing has not only generated strong returns for its clients but also played a role in creating a more sustainable and responsible business environment. The company's commitment to ESG investing practices has been a key driver of its long-term success and has made a meaningful positive impact on the world.

Case Study 3: Vanguard ESG U.S. Stock ETF

ESGV stands for Vanguard ESG U.S. Stock ETF, an exchange-traded fund (ETF) that aims to track the performance of companies selected based on environmental, social, and governance (ESG) criteria. ESG investing is socially responsible investing focusing on companies that positively impact the environment, society, and governance. The

ETF is a way to invest in a diversified portfolio of companies that meet these criteria rather than having to select individual stocks.

Vanguard incorporates ESG practices into its ETF by using a proprietary process to screen and select the companies included in the fund. This process involves evaluating companies based on ESG criteria, such as their environmental impact, labor practices, and corporate governance. Companies that score well on these criteria are more likely to be included in the fund. In contrast, those that score poorly may be excluded or given a lower weighting in the portfolio. Vanguard also uses data from external research providers. In addition, it engages with companies through voting and engagement activities to ensure they meet the standards.

as of 12/31/2022

	1-yr	3-yr	5-yr	10-yr	Since inception 09/18/2018
ESGV (Market price)	-24.05%	20.70%	--	--	38.88%
ESGV (NAV)	-24.02%	20.74%	--	--	38.90%
Benchmark[1]	-23.99%	21.04%	--	--	--

A table with Vanguard's ESGV ETF returns over a 1, 3, 5, and ten year period.
Source: Vanguard

Vanguard's ESG U.S. Stock ETF, like other funds that focus on socially responsible investing, has slightly lower returns than its benchmark (FTSE US All Cap Choice Index), demonstrating a 20.70% compared to the benchmark's 21.04% over three years. This is because the fund is selecting companies based on a set of ESG criteria, which may exclude some companies with higher financial returns but do not meet the criteria for ESG investing.

However, the slightly lower returns may be offset by the positive impact that the fund's ESG investment strategy can have on the world around us. By investing in companies that are committed to environmental and social responsibility, the fund can help promote sustainable business practices and contribute to the development of a more sustainable economy. Additionally, by avoiding companies that engage in unethical or environmentally harmful practices, the fund can help reduce the negative impact of these practices on society and the planet.

In summary, while Vanguard's ESG U.S. Stock ETF may have slightly lower returns compared to some benchmark indexes, it is important to consider the positive impact of the fund's ESG investment strategy on the world around us.

Best Practices for Implementing ESG Investing

ESG (environmental, social, and governance) investing is a growing trend in finance, as more and more investors are becoming conscious of their investments' environmental and social impact. This form of investing focuses on companies with strong environmental, social, and governance practices and working towards sustainability. To successfully navigate the world of ESG investing, it is important to understand the key principles and best practices. This section will discuss five of the most important best practices for ESG investing, including understanding the companies you are investing in, diversifying your investments, considering the long-term, engaging with companies, and monitoring and assessing your investments.

Understand the Companies You Are Investing In

Understanding the companies you are investing in is one of the most important aspects of ESG investing. Before investing, it is crucial to conduct thorough research and due diligence on the company to understand its exposure to environmental, social, and governance (ESG) risks. This research should include evaluating the company's environmental impact, labor practices, and corporate governance structure. By understanding the company's ESG risks and opportunities, investors can make informed decisions about whether or not to invest and how to engage with the company to encourage positive change.

When evaluating a company's environmental impact, it is important to consider factors such as its carbon footprint, energy usage, and water consumption. Investors should also look at the company's efforts to reduce their environmental impact and their plans for addressing climate change. Additionally, investors should assess the company's labor practices, including their treatment of employees and their efforts to promote diversity, equity, and inclusion in the workplace.

Corporate governance is another important aspect when evaluating a company's ESG risks. Investors should look at the company's leadership and management structure, including their board of directors and executive leadership team. They should also assess the company's transparency, accountability, and commitment to ethical business practices. By understanding the company's corporate governance structure, investors can identify any potential red flags or areas for improvement.

In conclusion, understanding the companies you invest in is a key aspect of ESG investing. By evaluating the company's environmental impact, labor practices, and corporate governance structure, investors can identify the company's ESG risks and opportunities and make informed decisions about whether or not to invest and how to engage with the company to encourage positive change.

Diversify Your Investments

One of the key investing principles is diversification, which is the strategy of spreading your investments across various sectors, industries, and geographies. The idea behind this is to reduce the overall risk of your portfolio by not putting all of your eggs in one basket.

This is especially important when investing in companies that align with environmental, social, and governance (ESG) criteria. ESG investing involves investing in companies with strong corporate governance practices that positively impact the environment and society.

However, it's important to note that not all companies or sectors are created equal regarding ESG risks. For example, companies in the oil and gas sector may be more exposed to environmental risks than those in the renewable energy sector. Similarly, companies in the consumer goods sector may be more exposed to human rights risks than those in the healthcare sector.

By diversifying your investments across different sectors and industries, you can reduce the overall risk of your portfolio and increase your chances of achieving long-term financial success. Additionally, by investing in companies across different geographies, you can reduce your portfolio risk by not relying too heavily on any one country or region.

In summary, diversifying your investments is a crucial strategy for reducing overall portfolio risk, especially in ESG investing. It's important to consider the specific ESG risks associated with different sectors and industries and to invest in various companies across different geographies to minimize risk.

Consider the Long-Term

Adopting a long-term perspective on environmental, social, and governance (ESG) investing is essential. This is because the benefits of ESG investing may not be immediately apparent and may take several years to materialize fully. Therefore, it is crucial to focus on a company's long-term potential and ability to effectively manage and navigate the various ESG risks it may face rather than just its short-term performance.

To ensure that a company is well-positioned to meet the evolving demands of responsible investing, it is important to consider its track record and commitment to ESG principles. It is also important to assess the company's plans for the future to ensure that it is taking steps to address any potential ESG risks and opportunities.

A wise old owl perched atop a towering oak tree deep in thought.

Furthermore, it is also important to consider the broader societal and environmental trends that may impact a company's long-term success. For example, the increasing focus on sustainability and shifting towards a low-carbon economy will likely significantly impact many industries. Therefore, considering how a company is positioning itself to navigate these challenges.

Overall, taking a long-term perspective on ESG investing is crucial for achieving the fullest potential of your investment. It is important to consider a company's current performance, long-term potential, and ability to adapt to the changing landscape of responsible investing. By taking a long-term view and carefully evaluating a company's ESG risks and opportunities, investors can make more informed decisions and increase the chances of achieving their desired investment outcomes.

Engage With Companies

As a shareholder, you can play a crucial role in promoting environmental, social, and governance (ESG) practices within the companies you invest in. One effective way to do this is by actively engaging with the companies.

One way to engage with companies is by participating in shareholder meetings and casting your vote on proposals related to ESG issues. This can include voting on resolutions related to environmental impact, labor rights, and ethical business practices. Using your voting power as a shareholder, you can help influence the company's direction and push for more sustainable and responsible practices.

Another way to engage with companies is communicating directly with management and board members. This can include sending letters or emails, attending town hall meetings, or setting up one-on-one meetings. By communicating directly with the company's people, you can share your concerns and suggestions for improving ESG practices. You can also ask questions and seek clarification on the company's current policies and plans.

Finally, you can join or form shareholder groups focused on ESG issues. These groups are made up of shareholders who share similar concerns and goals. Together, these shareholders can take collective action, such as filing shareholder resolutions, organizing campaigns and events, and engaging with other stakeholders. By joining or forming a shareholder group, you can amplify your voice and work with others to drive change within the company.

In summary, you can encourage companies to improve their ESG practices as a shareholder. You can vote on ESG-related proposals by engaging with companies, communicating directly with management and board members, and joining or forming shareholder groups focused on ESG issues. Together, these actions can help to create a more sustainable and responsible business environment.

Monitor and Assess Your Investments

Properly monitoring and assessing your investments is paramount if you wish to ensure that they align with your environmental, social, and governance (ESG) values and goals. This process involves a variety of tasks, such as tracking the performance of the companies in which you have invested on ESG issues, evaluating any changes in the leadership or business strategy of these companies, and staying informed about any material events or developments that may impact the ESG risk profile of the company.

For example, you should monitor the companies' adherence to environmental regulations, labor rights policies, and approaches to corporate governance. Investors can do this by keeping an eye on their annual reports, sustainability reports, and other relevant documents. You should also pay attention to any news or developments that may impact the company's reputation, such as lawsuits, scandals, or major management changes.

Furthermore, keeping track of changes in the company's leadership, business strategy, and overall financial performance is important. For instance, a change in the CEO or the company's board of directors may impact the company's ESG performance. Similarly, if the company announces a major acquisition or divestiture, it may affect its ESG risk profile.

Finally, it is essential to know material events or developments that may impact the company's ESG risk profile. For instance, a natural disaster, a change in government regulations, or a major industry disruption may significantly impact the company's performance and ESG risks.

Monitoring and assessing your investments regularly is crucial for ensuring they align with your ESG values and goals. By keeping track of the companies' performance on ESG issues, evaluating any changes in the company's leadership or business strategy, and being aware of any material events or developments that may impact the company's ESG risk profile, you can make informed decisions and optimize your portfolio.

In conclusion, ESG investing is a crucial aspect of responsible investing, focusing on companies that align with environmental, social, and governance criteria. It is important to understand the companies you are investing in by conducting thorough research and due diligence on the company's environmental impact, labor practices, and corporate governance structure. Diversifying your investments across different sectors, industries, and geographies is a key strategy for reducing overall portfolio risk. Additionally, adopting a long-term perspective on ESG investing is essential as the benefits may take several years to materialize fully. By following these principles, investors can make informed decisions, minimize risk, and achieve long-term financial success while promoting positive environmental and societal change.

The Role of Investors, Asset Managers, and Other Stakeholders in Advancing ESG Investing

The advancement of environmental, social, and governance (ESG) investing is a collective effort that involves multiple stakeholders. Investors, as the primary drivers of the capital market, play a crucial role in promoting ESG investing. By incorporating ESG factors into their investment decisions, they are signaling to companies that robust ESG practices are not only socially responsible but also financially beneficial.

Asset managers also play a vital role in advancing ESG investing by providing products and services that cater to the growing demand for sustainable investing. They can offer investment options that align with the values and goals of socially conscious investors and also help to educate them about the benefits of ESG investing.

Regulators also significantly advance ESG investing by creating a supportive framework that promotes transparency, disclosure, and accountability for ESG performance. They can also establish standards and guidelines that ensure companies are held accountable for their ESG performance.

Non-governmental organizations (NGOs) also play an important role in advancing ESG investing by providing education, resources, and advocacy for sustainable investing. In addition, they can work with investors and asset managers to raise awareness about the benefits of

ESG investing and help shape policy and regulatory frameworks that support sustainable investing.

Overall, advancing ESG investing requires the collective effort of investors, asset managers, regulators, and NGOs. Each stakeholder is critical in promoting sustainable investing and creating a more responsible and sustainable capital market.

In conclusion, ESG investing is a complex and rapidly growing field. Still, by understanding the practical aspects of ESG investing, investors can meaningfully incorporate these considerations into their investment strategies. This chapter has explored case studies of successful ESG investing strategies, best practices for implementing ESG investing in different asset classes and investment styles, and the role of investors, asset managers, and other stakeholders in advancing ESG investing. By understanding these aspects, investors can make more informed and sustainable investment decisions.

Chapter Summary

- ESG investing is a rapidly growing field, with more and more investors recognizing the potential benefits of incorporating these considerations into their investment strategies.
- Case studies of successful ESG investing strategies demonstrate the financial potential of investing in companies with strong ESG practices.
- Understanding the companies, you are investing in is a key aspect of ESG investing.
- Diversifying your investments is a crucial strategy for reducing overall portfolio risk, especially in ESG investing.
- Adopting a long-term perspective when it comes to ESG investing is essential.

- As a shareholder, you can play a crucial role in promoting ESG practices within the companies you invest in by engaging with them.
- Properly monitoring and assessing your investments is paramount if you wish to ensure that they align with your ESG values and goals.
- The advancement of ESG investing is a collective effort that involves multiple stakeholders, including investors, asset managers, regulators, and NGOs.

EPILOGUE

In conclusion, ESG investing has become an increasingly important topic in the investment community. By considering environmental, social, and governance factors in investment decisions, investors can positively impact society and the planet and improve financial performance. This book has discussed various aspects of ESG investing, including integrating ESG considerations into investment strategy, measuring and evaluating ESG performance, and understanding the role of regulators and government in ESG investing. Additionally, we have explored the relationship between ESG investing and financial performance and practical examples of ESG investing in practice. Overall, it is clear that ESG investing is a complex and evolving field. Still, by understanding the key principles and best practices outlined in this book, investors can make informed decisions that align with their values and financial goals.

The Benefits of ESG Investing for Sustainability and Positive Impact

Integrating environmental, social, and governance (ESG) considerations into investment decisions is crucial for achieving sustainable financial returns and promoting positive social and environmental change. ESG investing is a holistic approach that looks beyond traditional financial metrics to assess the long-term sustainability of a company or organization.

By considering ESG factors, investors can identify potential risks and opportunities that may not be visible through traditional financial analysis. This can lead to a more diversified and resilient investment portfolio, better equipped to navigate the complex and rapidly changing business landscape.

Furthermore, ESG investing is a powerful tool for promoting positive social and environmental change. By directing investment capital towards companies and organizations that prioritize sustainability, investors can play a key role in driving the transition towards a more just and sustainable society.

In addition, research has shown that companies with strong ESG performance tend to have better risk-adjusted returns and higher growth potential than their peers. This is because companies with sustainable business practices are more likely to be able to adapt and thrive in an uncertain future.

In conclusion, ESG investing is not only a responsible and ethical approach to investing but also a practical and profitable one. By considering ESG factors, investors can achieve sustainable financial returns while promoting positive social and environmental change.

The Ongoing Evolution of ESG Investing and Future Opportunities for Growth

Environmental, social, and governance (ESG) investing has undergone significant evolution in recent years and is expected to continue growing. ESG investing is an approach to investment that considers the impact of a company or organization on the environment, society, and corporate governance when making investment decisions.

The ongoing evolution of ESG investing has been driven by a growing awareness of the need to address pressing social and environmental issues, such as climate change and inequality, as well as a recognition that companies with strong ESG performance tend to have better risk-adjusted returns and higher growth potential.

One of the key trends in ESG investing is the increasing demand for data and transparency. Investors seek more information on how companies manage ESG risks and opportunities. Companies are responding by providing more ESG-related data and disclosures.

Another trend is the growing interest in impact investing, which focuses on investing in companies and organizations working to achieve specific social or environmental outcomes. Impact investing is an effective way for investors to align their values and financial goals. As a result, it is expected to continue growing in popularity.

ESG investing also has future opportunities for growth as many investors have an increased understanding of the materiality of ESG issues on their investment portfolios and its potential impact on long-term returns. As a result, more institutional investors are incorporating ESG factors into their investment decisions. Moreover, there is growing pressure from stakeholders, such as governments and consumers, for companies to improve their ESG performance.

In conclusion, ESG investing is an ongoing evolution, and the field is expected to grow. As investors become more aware of the materiality of ESG issues in their portfolios, they become more interested in incorporating ESG considerations into their investment decisions. This trend is expected to continue, providing more opportunities for growth in the ESG investing space.

THE POWER OF IMPACT INVESTING

A GUIDEBOOK FOR STRATEGIES, SECTORS, SUSTAINABLE DEVELOPMENT GOALS, SOCIAL ENTREPRENEURSHIP, CORPORATE SOCIAL RESPONSIBILITY, AND MORE

INTRODUCTION

Impact investing is a powerful tool that can help create positive social and environmental change while generating financial returns. This chapter will explore the definition, history, importance, types, and key players of impact investing.

Definition of Impact Investing

Impact investing is a relatively new concept that has gained significant traction recently. It is a form of investment that goes beyond the traditional focus on financial returns and instead prioritizes **social and environmental impact.** The goal of impact investing is to create positive change in the world while still earning a profit.

The concept of impact investing is rooted in the belief that businesses are responsible for contributing to society and the environment. Therefore, impact investors seek out companies committed to positively impacting and willing to support them financially. This can take many forms, from investing in renewable energy projects to funding education initiatives in underserved communities.

One of the key features of impact investing is the emphasis on measuring and reporting on social and environmental outcomes.

Impact investors want to see tangible evidence that their investments are making a difference, and they use a variety of metrics to track progress. This includes everything from carbon emissions reductions to improvements in health outcomes for disadvantaged populations.

Impact investing is not just for wealthy individuals or institutional investors. There are now a growing number of impact investment funds and platforms that allow everyday investors to participate. This democratization of impact investing can drive even greater positive change as more people become aware of the power of their investments to make a difference.

Overall, impact investing is a powerful tool for creating positive change in the world. By aligning financial goals with social and environmental objectives, impact investors can help address some of society's most pressing challenges. Whether you are an individual investor or a large institution, there are many opportunities to get involved in impact investing and make a difference.

History of Impact Investing

The concept of impact investing has been around for decades, tracing back to the 1960s. During this time, socially responsible investing emerged as a way for individuals to align their investments with personal values. This approach was driven by a desire to invest in companies that positively impacted society, such as being environmentally friendly or promoting social justice.

However, it was in the 1980s that the idea of impact investing began to take shape. This was when microfinance institutions started to provide small loans to low-income individuals and entrepreneurs in developing countries. These loans were designed to help people start or grow their businesses. They quickly became a powerful tool for poverty reduction.

As the microfinance industry grew, so too did the idea of **impact investing.** Investors began to see the potential for using their money to impact society while positively generating financial returns. This led to the development of the impact investing industry in the 2000s, which has since become a major force in finance.

Today, impact investing is a rapidly growing field encompassing many investment strategies and approaches. From investing in renewable energy projects to supporting social enterprises, impact investors use their money to drive positive change in the world. And as the world faces increasingly complex social and environmental challenges, the importance of impact investing is only set to grow.

Importance of Impact Investing

Impact investing is a crucial tool in the fight against social and environmental challenges that have plagued our world for decades. It is a powerful means of mobilizing private capital to address issues that governments and philanthropy alone cannot solve. By investing in companies and organizations that prioritize social and environmental impact, impact investors can help create a more sustainable and equitable future for all.

One of the most significant benefits of impact investing is its ability to generate financial returns for investors while simultaneously **creating positive social and environmental outcomes.** This is achieved by investing in companies committed to making a difference in the world through sustainable business practices, social entrepreneurship, or innovative solutions to pressing global issues.

Moreover, impact investing can help create new markets, products, and services that benefit society and the environment. By investing in companies developing new technologies or business models that prioritize sustainability and social impact, impact investors can help drive innovation and progress in these areas.

Another key advantage of impact investing is its potential to drive **systemic change.** By investing in companies and organizations that are working to address systemic issues such as poverty, inequality, and climate change, impact investors can help create a more just and sustainable world. Businesses can achieve this by supporting social and environmental justice initiatives, such as community development projects, renewable energy initiatives, and sustainable agriculture programs.

In conclusion, impact investing is critical for creating positive social and environmental outcomes while generating financial returns for investors. In addition, by investing in companies and organizations that prioritize sustainability and social impact, impact investors can help drive innovation, create new markets, and promote systemic change. As such, impact investing is essential to any strategy to create a more just and sustainable future for all.

Types of Impact Investing

Impact investing is a rapidly growing field that has gained significant traction recently. It is a form of investing that seeks to generate positive social and environmental outcomes alongside financial returns. There are several types of impact investing, each with unique characteristics, risks, and opportunities.

One of the most popular forms of impact investing is **social impact bonds**. These financial instruments allow investors to fund social programs and initiatives that address specific social issues, such as homelessness, education, or healthcare. Social impact bonds are structured, so investors receive a return on their investment only if the program achieves its predetermined social outcomes.

Another type of impact investing is **green bonds**. These fixed-income securities fund environmentally friendly projects, such as renewable energy, energy efficiency, or sustainable agriculture. Green bonds are becoming increasingly popular as investors seek to align their investments with their values and support the transition to a low-carbon economy.

Community investing is another form of impact investing focusing on providing capital to underserved communities and businesses. This type of investing aims to promote economic development and social equity by supporting small businesses, affordable housing, and community facilities in low-income areas.

Microfinance is another type of impact investing that provides financial services, such as loans, savings, and insurance, to low-income individuals and communities. Microfinance institutions aim to promote financial inclusion and empower individuals to improve their livelihoods and break the cycle of poverty.

Finally, **venture philanthropy** is a form of impact investing that combines the principles of venture capital with philanthropy. Venture philanthropists invest in social enterprises and nonprofits that have the potential to generate significant social impact and financial returns. They provide financial, strategic, and operational support to help these organizations achieve their goals.

In conclusion, impact investing offers a range of opportunities for investors to generate positive social and environmental outcomes alongside financial returns. By understanding the different types of impact investing and their unique characteristics, investors can choose the approach that best aligns with their values and investment goals.

Key Players in Impact Investing

The world of impact investing is a complex and multifaceted ecosystem comprising a diverse range of key players. These players include impact investors, social entrepreneurs, philanthropists, foundations, development finance institutions, and governments. Each of these players has a unique role in advancing the field of impact investing and achieving positive social and environmental outcomes.

Impact investors are individuals or organizations that invest in companies or projects to generate a measurable social or environmental impact alongside a financial return. They are often motivated by a desire to create positive change in the world and to use their capital to address pressing social and environmental challenges.

Social entrepreneurs, on the other hand, are individuals or organizations that use business models to create social or environmental impact. They are often driven by a desire to solve a specific social or environmental problem and to create sustainable solutions that can be scaled and replicated.

Philanthropists and foundations also play a critical role in impact investing. They provide funding and support to social entrepreneurs and impact investors, often focusing on specific issues such as education, healthcare, or the environment. They also help to build the infrastructure and networks needed to support the growth of the impact investing field.

Development finance institutions, such as the World Bank or the International Finance Corporation, are specialized organizations that provide financing and technical assistance to support economic development in developing countries. They often work closely with impact investors and social entrepreneurs to help them access the capital and resources they need to scale their impact.

Finally, **governments** also have an important role to play in impact investing. They can create policies and regulations that support the growth of the impact investing field, such as tax incentives or impact reporting requirements. They can also provide funding and support for social entrepreneurs and impact investors, particularly in areas where the private sector may be hesitant to invest.

In summary, the impact investing ecosystem comprises diverse key players, each with a unique role in advancing the field and achieving positive social and environmental outcomes. These players can help create a more just and sustainable world by working together.

In conclusion, impact investing is a powerful tool that can help create positive social and environmental change while generating financial returns. By understanding the definition, history, importance, types, and key players of impact investing, we can become more informed and engaged investors who can make a difference in the world.

1

UNDERSTANDING IMPACT INVESTING

A tree growing out of a piggy bank, symbolizing the positive impact of investing in sustainable agriculture.

Impact investing is a rapidly growing field that seeks to create positive social and environmental outcomes while generating financial returns. It is a powerful tool for investors who want to align their investments with their values and make a difference in the world. In this chapter, we will explore the principles of impact investing, the importance of impact measurement and evaluation, the risks and challenges of impact investing, how it differs from traditional investing, and the unique opportunities and challenges of impact investing in developing countries.

Principles of Impact Investing

Impact investing is a unique approach to investing that is guided by a set of principles that distinguish it from traditional investing. These principles are intentionality, additionality, measurability, and accountability. Let's take a closer look at each of these principles.

Intentionality is a key principle of impact investing. It means that investors seek to create positive social and environmental outcomes alongside financial returns. In other words, impact investors focus on making money rather than positively impacting the world. This is a fundamental difference between impact investing and traditional investing.

Another important principle of impact investing is **additionality**. This means that impact investments should not displace existing funding sources but instead provide new capital to address unmet needs. Impact investors are looking to fill gaps in the market and provide funding to projects that might not otherwise receive it.

Measurability is also a critical principle of impact investing. Investors should track and report on their investments' social and environmental outcomes. This is important because it allows investors to see the impact of their investments and make adjustments as needed. Measuring impact is not always easy, but ensuring that investments make a positive difference is essential.

Finally, **accountability** is a key principle of impact investing.

Investors should be transparent about their impact and accountable to their stakeholders. This means that impact investors should be open about their investments and the impact they are having. They should also be accountable to the communities they are investing in and ensure that their investments align with the needs and priorities of those communities.

To be effective, impact investors must also consider the context in which they invest. This means understanding the social, economic, and environmental factors affecting the communities they invest in. It also means engaging with stakeholders, including the communities, to ensure that investments align with their needs and priorities. Finally, impact investors must be aware of their investments' impact and be willing to make changes if necessary.

In conclusion, impact investing is a unique approach to investing that is guided by a set of principles that distinguish it from traditional investing. These principles include intentionality, additionality, measurability, and accountability. To be effective, impact investors must also consider the context in which they invest and engage with stakeholders to ensure that their investments align with the needs and priorities of the communities they are investing in.

Impact Measurement and Evaluation

In today's world, investing is **not just about financial returns.** Investors are increasingly looking for ways to impact society and the environment positively. Impact investing is a growing trend seeking to generate financial returns and positive social and environmental outcomes. However, measuring and evaluating the impact of these investments is critical to their success.

Impact measurement and evaluation allow investors to understand their investments' social and environmental outcomes. As a result, it helps them make informed decisions about future investments and ensures that their investments are making a positive impact. However, measuring impact can be challenging, as social and environmental outcomes are often difficult to quantify and measure.

To address this challenge, impact investors use various tools and frameworks. One such tool is the **Impact Management Project**, which provides a standardized approach to measuring and managing impact. It helps investors define and measure impact, set targets and benchmarks, and report on their progress.

Another tool is the **Global Impact Investing Network's Impact Reporting and Investment Standards**. This framework provides guidelines for impact investors to report on their investments' social and environmental outcomes. It helps investors communicate their impact to stakeholders and ensures transparency and accountability.

Finally, the **United Nations Sustainable Development Goals** provide a framework for investors to align their investments with global sustainability goals. The SDGs provide a set of 17 goals and 169 targets that address social, economic, and environmental issues. By aligning their investments with these goals, investors can ensure they positively impact society and the environment.

In conclusion, measuring and evaluating the impact of investments is critical to the success of impact investing. Impact investors use various tools and frameworks to address the challenge of measuring impact, including the Impact Management Project, the Global Impact Investing Network's Impact Reporting and Investment Standards, and the United Nations Sustainable Development Goals. Using these tools, investors can ensure that their investments positively impact society and the environment.

Risks and Challenges of Impact Investing

Impact investing is a unique strategy to generate positive social and environmental outcomes and financial returns. However, like any investment, it carries risks that must be carefully considered and managed. These risks can be broadly categorized into financial, social, and environmental.

Financial risks are the most obvious risks associated with impact investing. As with any investment, there is always the possibility of losing money. Therefore, impact investors must carefully evaluate the financial viability of their investments and ensure that they are making sound financial decisions. This requires a thorough understanding of the market, the investment opportunity, and the potential risks and rewards.

In addition to financial risks, impact investors must consider **social and environmental risks.** These risks can arise when the intended positive impact of an investment is not realized or when unintended negative consequences occur. For example, investing in a renewable energy project may have unintended negative consequences for local communities if it displaces people from their homes or disrupts traditional livelihoods.

To mitigate these risks, impact investors must conduct thorough due diligence before making investment decisions. This involves researching the investment opportunity, assessing the potential risks and rewards, and engaging with stakeholders to understand their perspectives and concerns. Impact investors must also be willing to adapt their strategies as needed to ensure they achieve their intended social and environmental outcomes.

Working in complex social and environmental contexts can also present challenges for impact investors. For example, addressing systemic issues like poverty and climate change requires a long-term, collaborative approach that involves multiple stakeholders. Impact investors must be able to navigate these complex contexts and build strong partnerships with other investors, governments, and civil society organizations.

In conclusion, impact investing carries risks that must be carefully considered and managed. However, impact investors can mitigate these risks by conducting thorough due diligence, engaging with stakeholders, building strong partnerships, and achieving their intended social and environmental outcomes. Ultimately, impact investing has the potential to generate positive change in the world while also generating financial returns for investors.

Impact Investing vs. Traditional Investing

When it comes to investing, there are two main approaches: **traditional investing** and **impact investing**. While both aim to generate returns on investment, their priorities and methods differ.

Traditional investing is primarily focused on financial returns. Investors seek to maximize profits by investing in companies and assets expected to perform well in the short term. This approach often relies on financial metrics, such as return on investment, to measure success.

In contrast, impact investing seeks to create positive social and environmental outcomes alongside financial returns. This means that impact investors prioritize investments that positively impact society and the environment and generate financial returns. In addition, impact investing takes a longer-term view, recognizing that social and environmental change often requires sustained effort over time.

While traditional and impact investing may seem like opposing approaches, they are not mutually exclusive. For example, many impact investors use traditional investment strategies, such as diversification and risk management, alongside impact-focused strategies. This allows them to generate financial returns while also making a positive impact on society and the environment.

One of the key differences between traditional and impact investing is the metrics used to measure success. Traditional investing tends to focus on financial metrics, such as return on investment and earnings per share. Impact investing, on the other hand, uses broader metrics, including social and environmental impact. This means that impact investors may prioritize investments that positively impact issues such as climate change, poverty, and inequality, even if they may not generate the highest financial returns in the short term.

Overall, impact investing represents a shift in how we think about investing. It recognizes that financial returns are not the only measure of success and that investors are responsible for considering their investments' impact on society and the environment. While impact investing is still a relatively new approach, it has the potential to drive positive change and create a more sustainable and equitable future.

Impact Investing in Developing Countries

Impact investing in developing countries is a complex and multifaceted endeavor that requires a deep understanding of these countries' unique opportunities and challenges. On the one hand, developing countries often face significant social and environmental challenges that impact investors can help address. These challenges may include poverty, lack of access to basic services such as healthcare and education, and environmental degradation.

However, investing in developing countries also comes with its own set of challenges. These countries often have complex political and economic contexts that make investing challenging. For example, corruption, weak governance, and unstable economies can all pose significant risks to investors.

To be effective in developing countries, impact investors must be willing to put in the time and effort to **understand the local context**. This means engaging with local stakeholders, including community members, government officials, and civil society organizations. By building strong partnerships with local organizations, impact investors can better understand the needs and priorities of the communities they are working with.

In addition, impact investors must be willing to take a long-term view and be patient in achieving their impact goals. Creating sustainable change in developing countries often takes time and requires a deep commitment to the communities being served. Therefore, impact investors must be willing to invest in projects and initiatives that may yield little results but that have the potential to create lasting change over time.

Ultimately, impact investing in developing countries is a powerful tool for creating positive social and environmental change. By understanding the unique opportunities and challenges these countries present, impact investors can make a meaningful difference in the lives of millions of people worldwide.

. . .

Impact investing is a powerful tool for investors who want to create positive social and environmental outcomes while generating financial returns. However, to be effective, impact investors must be guided by a set of principles that distinguish them from traditional investing, measure and evaluate their impact, navigate risks and challenges, understand the differences between impact investing and traditional investing, and be willing to adapt their strategies to the unique opportunities and challenges of investing in developing countries.

Chapter Summary

- Impact investing is guided by principles that distinguish it from traditional investing.
- Measuring and evaluating impact is critical to the success of impact investing.
- Impact investing carries financial, social, and environmental risks.
- Impact investing differs from traditional investing in its focus on social and environmental outcomes.
- Impact investing in developing countries presents unique opportunities and challenges.
- Impact investors must understand the local context and engage with local stakeholders.
- Impact investors must take a long-term view and be patient in achieving their impact goals.
- Impact investing and traditional investing are not mutually exclusive.

2

IMPACT INVESTING STRATEGIES

A tree with roots deeply entrenched in the earth, symbolizing the long-term impact of sustainable investing strategies.

Impact investing is a growing trend in the investment world. Investors seek to positively impact society and the environment while earning a financial return. Impact investing strategies are diverse, ranging from socially responsible investing to microfinance. This chapter will explore five impact investing strategies that are gaining popularity: socially responsible investing, environmental, social, and governance (ESG) investing, community investing, microfinance, and impact bonds. We will discuss the benefits and challenges of each strategy and provide examples of successful impact investments.

Socially Responsible Investing

Socially responsible investing (SRI) is an investment strategy considering financial return and social and environmental impact. SRI investors seek to invest in companies that align with their values and avoid companies that engage in harmful practices. Investors can achieve SRI through negative screening, positive screening, or shareholder advocacy. Negative screening involves excluding companies that engage in activities such as tobacco, weapons, or fossil fuels. Positive screening involves investing in companies that positively impact society and the environment, such as renewable energy or sustainable agriculture. Finally, shareholder advocacy involves using shareholder power to influence corporate behavior.

SRI has gained popularity recently, with more investors seeking to align their investments with their values. SRI funds have also performed well, with some outperforming traditional funds. However, SRI has challenges, such as defining socially responsible behavior and balancing financial return with social and environmental impact. Despite these challenges, SRI is a powerful tool for investors to impact society and the environment positively.

Environmental, Social, and Governance (ESG) Investing

ESG investing is an investment strategy that considers environmental, social, and governance factors in addition to financial return. ESG investors seek to invest in companies that positively impact society and the environment and are well-governed. ESG factors include climate change, human rights, labor standards, board diversity, and executive compensation. ESG investing can be achieved through integration, engagement, or impact investing. Integration involves incorporating ESG factors into traditional investment analysis. Engagement involves using shareholder power to influence corporate behavior. Impact investing involves investing in companies or projects with a specific social or environmental impact.

ESG investing has gained popularity in recent years, with more investors recognizing the importance of considering non-financial factors in investment decisions. ESG funds have also performed well, with some outperforming traditional funds. However, ESG has its challenges, such as defining ESG factors and measuring their impact. Despite these challenges, ESG is a powerful tool for investors to impact society and the environment positively.

Suppose you're interested in learning more about ESG investing. In that case, you can find my other book, *"The Power of ESG Investing,"* at your favorite book retailer.

Community Investing

Community investing is an investment strategy that seeks to provide capital to underserved communities and support community development. Community investors invest in community development financial institutions (CDFIs) or other organizations that provide loans or other financial services to low-income communities. Community investing can support affordable housing, small business development, and job creation in underserved communities.

Community investing has a long history in the United States, with CDFIs providing critical support to low-income communities. Community investing has also gained popularity recently, with more investors recognizing the importance of supporting underserved communities. However, community investing has challenges, such as finding viable investment opportunities in underserved communities and balancing financial return with social impact. Despite these challenges, community investing is a powerful tool for investors to support community development and promote economic justice.

Microfinance

Microfinance is an investment strategy that provides small loans and other financial services to low-income individuals and small businesses in developing countries. Microfinance can support entrepreneurship, job creation, and poverty reduction in developing countries. Microfinance institutions (MFIs) provide loans, savings accounts, and other financial services to low-income individuals and small businesses.

Microfinance has gained popularity recently, with more investors recognizing the importance of supporting entrepreneurship and economic development in developing countries. Microfinance has also been successful in promoting financial inclusion and poverty reduction. However, microfinance has challenges, such as finding viable investment opportunities in developing countries and balancing financial return with social impact. Despite these challenges, microfinance is a powerful tool for investors to support economic development and promote financial inclusion in developing countries.

Impact Bonds

Impact bonds are a financing mechanism that provides funding for social or environmental programs based on their outcomes. Impact bonds involve a partnership between investors, service providers, and government agencies. Investors fund social or environmental programs, and service providers deliver the programs. If the programs achieve their desired outcomes, the government agency pays the investors a return.

Impact bonds have gained popularity in recent years, with more investors recognizing the importance of measuring social and environmental impact. Impact bonds have also successfully promoted innovation and collaboration in social and environmental programs. However, impact bonds have challenges, such as defining outcomes and measuring impact. Despite these challenges, impact bonds are a powerful tool for investors to support social and environmental programs and promote innovation and collaboration.

Impact investing strategies are diverse and powerful tools for investors to impact society and the environment positively. Each strategy has its benefits and challenges, but all can provide financial returns and social and environmental impact. By considering impact investing strategies, investors can align their investments with their values and support positive social and environmental change.

Chapter Summary

- Socially responsible investing considers financial return and social and environmental impact.
- Environmental, social, and governance (ESG) investing considers ESG factors in addition to financial return.
- Community investing provides capital to underserved communities and supports community development.
- Microfinance provides small loans and other financial services to low-income individuals and small businesses in developing countries.
- Impact bonds fund social or environmental programs based on their outcomes.
- SRI, ESG, community investing, microfinance, and impact bonds are powerful tools for investors to positively impact society and the environment.

- Impact investing strategies have benefits and challenges, but all can provide financial return and social and environmental impact.
- By considering impact investing strategies, investors can align their investments with their values and support positive social and environmental change.

3

IMPACT INVESTING SECTORS

A city skyline at night, with green energy solutions like wind turbines and solar panels prominently featured on rooftops.

Impact investing is a rapidly growing field that aims to generate positive social and environmental impact alongside financial returns. Impact investors seek to invest in companies and organizations making a difference worldwide. Several sectors are particularly popular for impact investing. This chapter will explore five sectors: education, healthcare, renewable energy, agriculture, and affordable housing. We will examine the impact investments in these sectors can have and highlight some of the most promising opportunities for impact investors.

Education

Investing in education is one of the most impactful ways to create positive change in the world. Education is the key to unlocking human potential and is essential for economic growth and social development. Impact investors can invest in various education-related initiatives, including schools, training programs, and educational technology companies.

Investments in education can have a wide range of positive impacts. For example, investing in schools can help to improve access to education for children in underserved communities. Investing in training programs can equip people with the skills they need to succeed in the workforce. And investing in educational technology companies can help to create innovative solutions that make learning more engaging and effective.

There are several promising opportunities for impact investors in the education sector. One example is investing in companies that provide affordable and accessible online education. Another example is investing in schools that serve low-income communities and provide high-quality education. As a result, impact investors can help create a brighter future for individuals and communities worldwide by investing in education.

Healthcare

Investing in healthcare is another impactful way to create positive change in the world. Access to healthcare is essential for human well-being and a key driver of economic growth and social development. Impact investors can invest in various healthcare-related initiatives, including hospitals, clinics, and medical technology companies.

Investments in healthcare can have a wide range of positive impacts. For example, investing in hospitals and clinics can help improve healthcare access for people in underserved communities. Investing in medical technology companies can help to create innovative solutions that improve the quality and efficiency of healthcare. Finally, investing in healthcare training programs can equip people with the skills they need to provide high-quality care.

There are several promising opportunities for impact investors in the healthcare sector. One example is investing in companies that provide affordable and accessible healthcare services. Another example is investing in medical technology companies developing innovative solutions to healthcare challenges. By investing in healthcare, impact investors can help improve the health and well-being of individuals and communities worldwide.

Renewable Energy

Investing in renewable energy is a powerful way to create positive change in the world. Renewable energy is essential for reducing greenhouse gas emissions and mitigating the impacts of climate change. Impact investors can invest in various renewable energy initiatives, including solar, wind, and hydroelectric power projects.

Investments in renewable energy can have a wide range of positive impacts. For example, investing in solar power projects can reduce reliance on fossil fuels and decrease greenhouse gas emissions. Investing in wind power projects can create jobs and stimulate economic growth in rural communities. And investing in hydroelectric power projects can help to provide clean energy to communities that lack access to electricity.

There are several promising opportunities for impact investors in the renewable energy sector. One example is investing in companies that develop and manufacture renewable energy technologies. Another example is investing in renewable energy projects that provide affordable and accessible energy to underserved communities. By investing in renewable energy, impact investors can help to create a more sustainable and equitable future for all.

Agriculture

Investing in agriculture is a powerful way to create positive change in the world. Agriculture is essential for food security and economic development and is a key social and environmental sustainability driver. Impact investors can invest in various agriculture-related initiatives, including sustainable farming practices, food processing and distribution, and agricultural technology companies.

Investments in agriculture can have a wide range of positive impacts. For example, investing in sustainable farming practices can help to improve soil health, reduce water usage, and increase crop yields. Investing in food processing and distribution can create jobs and stimulate economic growth in rural communities. And investing in agricultural technology companies can help to create innovative solutions that improve the efficiency and sustainability of agriculture.

There are several promising opportunities for impact investors in the agriculture sector. One example is investing in companies that develop and manufacture sustainable farming technologies. Another example is investing in food processing and distribution companies that prioritize social and environmental sustainability. By investing in agriculture, impact investors can help to create a more sustainable and equitable food system for all.

Affordable Housing

Investing in affordable housing is a powerful way to create positive change in the world. Access to safe and affordable housing is essential for human well-being and a key driver of economic growth and social development. Impact investors can invest in various affordable housing initiatives, including housing developments, community land trusts, and housing cooperatives.

Investments in affordable housing can have a wide range of positive impacts. For example, investing in affordable housing can help provide safe and stable housing for low-income families. Investing in community land trusts can help to create affordable housing that is permanently affordable and community-controlled. And investing in housing cooperatives can help to create a sense of community and shared ownership among residents.

There are several promising opportunities for impact investors in the affordable housing sector. One example is investing in affordable housing developments prioritizing social and environmental sustainability. Another example is investing in community land trusts prioritizing community control and resident participation. By investing in affordable housing, impact investors can help to create a more equitable and sustainable housing system for all.

Impact investing in education, healthcare, renewable energy, agriculture, and affordable housing can have a powerful and positive impact on individuals and communities worldwide. By investing in these sectors, impact investors can help to create a more sustainable, equitable, and prosperous future for all.

Chapter Summary

- Investing in education can improve access to education, training, and educational technology.

- Investing in healthcare can improve access to healthcare, medical technology, and training.
- Investing in renewable energy can reduce greenhouse gas emissions and provide clean energy to underserved communities.
- Investing in agriculture can improve soil health, increase crop yields, and create sustainable food systems.
- Investing in affordable housing can provide safe and stable housing for low-income families and create community-controlled housing.
- Promising opportunities for impact investors in education include affordable and accessible online education and schools that serve low-income communities.
- Promising opportunities for impact investors in healthcare include affordable and accessible healthcare services and medical technology companies that develop innovative solutions to healthcare challenges.
- Promising opportunities for impact investors in renewable energy, agriculture, and affordable housing include investing in sustainable technologies, community-controlled initiatives, and projects prioritizing social and environmental sustainability.

4

IMPACT INVESTING IN ACTION

A plant growing in a desert, symbolizing the transformative power of impact investing to turn seemingly barren or hopeless situations into thriving and sustainable communities.

Impact investing is a powerful tool to drive social and environmental change while generating financial returns. This chapter will explore the impact investing landscape and showcase successful case studies from the public and private sectors, philanthropy, and the nonprofit sector. We will also examine each sector's unique challenges and opportunities in implementing impact investing strategies. By the end of this chapter, you will have a deeper understanding of how impact investing can create positive change and how you can get involved.

Case Studies of Successful Impact Investments

Impact investing has the potential to create significant social and environmental impact while generating financial returns. In this section, we will explore some successful case studies that demonstrate the power of impact investing. One such example is the Acumen Fund, which invests in companies that provide essential goods and services to low-income communities in developing countries. Through its investments, Acumen has helped to improve millions of people's access to healthcare, education, and clean energy.

Another successful impact investment is the Social Investment Business, which provides loans and grants to social enterprises in the UK. Since its inception, the Social Investment Business has invested over £450 million in more than 3,500 social enterprises (Social Investment Business, 2022), creating jobs and improving the lives of people in local communities.

Individuals can also use impact investing to address environmental challenges. For example, the California Clean Energy Fund (CalCEF) is a nonprofit organization that invests in clean energy startups. CalCEF has helped to accelerate more than 750 startups across 40 programs (New Energy Nexus, 2023), creating jobs and reducing greenhouse gas emissions.

In addition to these examples, impact investing has also been used to address issues such as affordable housing, education, and financial inclusion. These case studies demonstrate the power of impact investing in creating positive change in various sectors.

Impact Investing in the Public Sector

The public sector has a critical role to play in impact investing. Governments can use their resources and regulatory powers to create an enabling environment for impact investing. For example, the UK government has created a social investment tax relief (SITR) scheme that provides tax incentives for individuals who invest in social enterprises.

Governments can also use impact investing to address social and environmental challenges. For example, the Green Investment Bank in the UK was established to invest in renewable energy projects and support the transition to a low-carbon economy.

In addition to these examples, impact investing can also be used to fund public services such as healthcare and education. By leveraging private capital, governments can improve the quality and accessibility of public services while reducing the burden on taxpayers.

Impact Investing in the Private Sector

The private sector has been a driving force behind the growth of impact investing. Private investors can use their capital to support companies creating positive social and environmental impacts. In addition, impact investing can help companies to attract and retain talent, enhance their brand reputation, and improve their bottom line.

One example of a successful impact investment in the private sector is Patagonia. This clothing company has made sustainability a core part of its business model. Patagonia has invested in sustainable agriculture, renewable energy, and fair labor practices. As a result, it has become a leader in the sustainable fashion industry.

Another example is Unilever, a multinational consumer goods company that has made sustainability a key part of its business strategy. Unilever has invested in renewable energy, sustainable agriculture, and water conservation and has set ambitious targets to reduce its environmental impact.

Impact Investing in Philanthropy

Philanthropy has long been a driver of social and environmental change. Impact investing provides philanthropists with a new tool to achieve their goals. Philanthropists can create sustainable solutions to social and environmental challenges by investing in social enterprises and other impact-driven organizations.

One example of a successful impact investment in philanthropy is the Omidyar Network, founded by eBay founder Pierre Omidyar and his wife, Pam Omidyar. The Omidyar Network invests in organizations that create positive social and environmental impacts, including education, financial inclusion, and human rights.

Another example is the Ford Foundation, which has led impact investing for many years. The Ford Foundation has invested in affordable housing, community development, and other initiatives that create positive social impact.

Impact Investing in the Nonprofit Sector

Nonprofit organizations can also benefit from impact investing. By leveraging private capital, nonprofits can expand their impact and achieve their mission more effectively. Impact investing can also help nonprofits to become more financially sustainable and reduce their reliance on traditional fundraising methods.

One example of a successful impact investment in the nonprofit sector is the Robin Hood Foundation, which invests in poverty-fighting organizations in New York City. The Robin Hood Foundation has invested in education, job training, and other initiatives that help to lift people out of poverty.

Another example is the Acumen Fund, which we discussed earlier. Acumen invests in social enterprises that provide essential goods and services to low-income communities in developing countries. Through its investments, Acumen has helped improve millions of people's lives.

Impact investing is a powerful tool to create positive social and environmental change while generating financial returns. By investing in companies and organizations that are creating impact, we can help to address some of the world's most pressing challenges. Whether you are a philanthropist, investor, or nonprofit leader, there are opportunities to get involved in impact investing and make a difference.

Chapter Summary

- Impact investing can create significant social and environmental impact while generating financial returns.
- Successful impact investments include the Acumen Fund, Social Investment Business, and California Clean Energy Fund.
- The public sector can use impact investing to address social and environmental challenges and fund public services.
- The private sector can use impact investing to support sustainable business practices and attract and retain talent.
- Philanthropy can use impact investing to create sustainable solutions to social and environmental challenges.
- Nonprofits can use impact investing in expanding their impact and becoming more financially sustainable.
- Impact investing can help to address issues such as affordable housing, education, and financial inclusion.
- There are opportunities for individuals and organizations to get involved in impact investing and make a difference.

5

IMPACT INVESTING AND SUSTAINABLE DEVELOPMENT GOALS

A tree growing out of a coin, symbolizing the impact investing can have on sustainable development goals, such as reforestation and biodiversity conservation.

Impact investing is a powerful tool investors can use to address some of the world's most pressing social and environmental challenges. One of the most powerful frameworks for addressing these challenges is the **United Nations' Sustainable Development Goals** (SDGs). The SDGs are 17 goals that aim to end poverty, protect the planet, and ensure prosperity for all. This chapter will explore the relationship between impact investing and the SDGs, focusing on four specific goals: No Poverty, Zero Hunger, Good Health and Well-being, and Quality Education. We will examine how impact investing can help achieve these goals and the opportunities and challenges associated.

Overview of Sustainable Development Goals

The Sustainable Development Goals were adopted by the United Nations in 2015 and are a universal call to action to end poverty, protect the planet, and ensure that all people enjoy peace and prosperity. The 17 goals are interconnected and address a range of issues, including poverty, hunger, health, education, gender equality, clean water and sanitation, affordable and clean energy, decent work and economic growth, industry, innovation and infrastructure, reduced inequalities, sustainable cities and communities, responsible consumption and production, climate action, life below water, life on land, peace, justice, and strong institutions, and partnerships for the goals.

SDG 1: No Poverty

SDG 1 aims to end poverty in all its forms, everywhere. Impact investing can be critical in achieving this goal by providing capital to businesses and organizations working to create economic opportunities for impoverished people. For example, impact investors can invest in microfinance institutions, social enterprises, and other organizations that provide financial services, job training, and other support to low-income communities. Impact investing can also help address the root causes of poverty by investing in businesses that create jobs, improve access to education and healthcare, and promote sustainable economic growth.

SDG 2: Zero Hunger

SDG 2 aims to end hunger, achieve food security and improved nutrition, and promote sustainable agriculture. Impact investing can help achieve this goal by investing in businesses that promote sustainable agriculture, improve food distribution systems, and increase access to nutritious food. Impact investors can also support organizations that provide training and education to farmers, promote sustainable farming practices, and increase access to markets for small-scale farmers.

SDG 3: Good Health and Well-being

SDG 3 aims to ensure healthy lives and promote well-being for all ages. Impact investing can help achieve this goal by investing in businesses that provide healthcare services, develop new medical technologies, and promote healthy lifestyles. Impact investors can also support organizations that provide education and training to healthcare workers, improve access to healthcare in underserved communities, and promote disease prevention and management.

SDG 4: Quality Education

SDG 4 aims to ensure inclusive and equitable education and promote lifelong learning opportunities for all. Impact investing can help achieve this goal by investing in businesses that provide education services, develop new educational technologies, and promote access to education for marginalized communities. Impact investors can also support organizations that provide teacher training, improve access to education in underserved communities, and promote education for girls and women.

Impact investing can play a significant role in achieving Sustainable Development Goals. By investing in businesses and organizations that are working to address poverty, hunger, health, and education, impact investors can help create positive social and environmental impacts while generating financial returns. However, impact investing has challenges, and investors must carefully consider their investments' social and environmental impact. Nevertheless, impact investors, businesses, and organizations can help create a more sustainable and equitable world by working together.

Chapter Summary

- The Sustainable Development Goals are 17 goals that aim to end poverty, protect the planet, and ensure prosperity for all.
- Impact investing can help achieve the SDGs by providing capital to businesses and organizations working to create positive social and environmental impact.
- Impact investing can help achieve SDG 1 by investing in businesses that create economic opportunities for impoverished people.
- Impact investing can help achieve SDG 2 by investing in businesses that promote sustainable agriculture and increase access to nutritious food.
- Impact investing can help achieve SDG 3 by investing in businesses that provide healthcare services and promote healthy lifestyles.
- Impact investing can help achieve SDG 4 by investing in businesses that provide education services and promote access to education for marginalized communities.

- Impact investing has challenges, and investors must carefully consider their investments' social and environmental impact.
- By working together, impact investors, businesses, and organizations can help create a more sustainable and equitable world.

6

IMPACT INVESTING AND SUSTAINABLE DEVELOPMENT GOALS (CONT.)

A futuristic cityscape powered by sustainable infrastructure, showcasing the impact investing sectors of green buildings, sustainable transportation, and waste management.

Impact investing is a powerful tool for achieving Sustainable Development Goals (SDGs). The previous chapter discussed how impact investing could contribute to SDGs 1-4. This chapter will explore how impact investing can help achieve SDGs 5-9. These goals are critical for creating a more equitable, sustainable, and prosperous world. By investing in companies and projects that align with these goals, impact investors can drive positive social and environmental change while generating financial returns.

SDG 5: Gender Equality

Gender equality is a fundamental human right for creating a peaceful, prosperous, and sustainable world. Impact investors can play a crucial role in promoting gender equality by investing in companies and projects that empower women and girls. Here are five ways that impact investing can contribute to SDG 5:

Firstly, impact investors can invest in women-led businesses. Women entrepreneurs often face significant barriers to accessing capital, markets, and networks. By investing in women-led businesses, impact investors can help bridge this gap and support positive social and environmental impact.

Secondly, impact investors can support women's health and well-being by investing in companies and projects that provide women access to healthcare, education, and other essential services. This can help improve women's health and well-being, which is critical for achieving gender equality.

Thirdly, impact investors can promote gender diversity and inclusion by encouraging companies to adopt gender diversity and inclusion policies and practices. This can help create a more equitable and inclusive workplace that benefits both women and men.

Fourthly, impact investors can address gender-based violence by investing in companies and projects tackling domestic violence, sexual harassment, and human trafficking. This can help create safer and more secure communities for women and girls.

Finally, impact investors can support women's economic empowerment by investing in companies and projects that provide women with access to financial services, training, and employment opportunities. This can help women achieve economic independence and contribute to their families and communities.

In conclusion, impact investing can be a powerful tool for promoting gender equality. By investing in companies and projects that empower women and girls, impact investors can help create a more just and equitable world.

SDG 6: Clean Water and Sanitation

Access to clean water and sanitation is a fundamental human right and a crucial foundation for sustainable development. Unfortunately, the global water crisis continues to threaten the health and well-being of millions worldwide. However, impact investors can play a vital role in addressing this crisis by investing in companies and projects that promote clean water and sanitation. Here are five ways impact investing can contribute to SDG 6:

Firstly, impact investors can invest in companies and projects that build and maintain water infrastructure, such as water treatment plants, pipelines, and storage facilities. By doing so, they can help ensure that communities have access to clean and safe water.

Secondly, impact investors can invest in companies and projects that promote water conservation, such as efficient irrigation systems, rainwater harvesting, and wastewater reuse. This can reduce water waste and ensure that water resources are used sustainably.

Thirdly, impact investors can invest in companies and projects that address water pollution, such as industrial wastewater treatment, river restoration, and marine conservation. This can help protect water quality and biodiversity.

Fourthly, impact investors can invest in companies and projects providing sanitation access, such as toilets, sewage treatment, and waste management. This can help improve public health and reduce the spread of waterborne diseases.

Lastly, impact investors can invest in water-related entrepreneurship, such as water filtration, desalination, and irrigation technologies. By doing so, they can create new business opportunities and promote innovation in the water sector.

In conclusion, impact investing can be crucial in addressing the global water crisis and promoting sustainable development. By investing in companies and projects promoting clean water and sanitation, impact investors can help ensure everyone has access to these basic human rights.

SDG 7: Affordable and Clean Energy

Access to affordable and clean energy is crucial for achieving sustainable development. Impact investors can significantly accelerate the transition to a low-carbon economy by investing in companies and projects promoting affordable and clean energy. Here are five ways impact investing can contribute to SDG 7:

Firstly, impact investors can invest in companies and projects that generate renewable energy, such as solar, wind, and hydropower. This can help reduce greenhouse gas emissions and promote energy independence. Furthermore, by investing in renewable energy, impact investors can support the development of sustainable energy sources that are both environmentally friendly and cost-effective.

Secondly, impact investors can invest in companies and projects that promote energy efficiency, such as building retrofits, smart grids, and energy storage. This can help reduce energy waste and lower energy costs. By supporting energy efficiency, impact investors can help businesses and households save money on their energy bills while reducing their carbon footprint.

Thirdly, impact investors can invest in companies and projects that provide access to affordable and clean energy for low-income communities, such as off-grid solar systems and mini-grids. This can help reduce energy poverty and improve the quality of life for those who lack access to reliable energy sources. Impact investors can help bridge the energy gap and promote social equity by investing in energy access.

Fourthly, impact investors can invest in companies and projects that promote sustainable transportation, such as electric vehicles, public transit, and bike-sharing. This can help reduce air pollution and traffic congestion, leading to cleaner and healthier cities. By supporting sustainable transportation, impact investors can help create a more sustainable future for urban areas.

Finally, impact investors can invest in energy-related entrepreneurship, such as energy storage, carbon capture, and biofuels. This can create new business opportunities and promote innovation in the energy sector. By supporting energy-related entrepreneurship, impact investors can help drive the development of new technologies and solutions that can help address the challenges of climate change.

In conclusion, impact investing can be critical in promoting sustainable development by investing in companies and projects promoting affordable and clean energy. By investing in renewable energy, energy efficiency, energy access, sustainable transportation, and energy-related entrepreneurship, impact investors can help accelerate the transition to a low-carbon economy and create a more sustainable future for all.

SDG 8: Decent Work and Economic Growth

Decent work and economic growth are crucial for reducing poverty and promoting sustainable development. Impact investors can create decent work and economic growth by investing in companies and projects prioritizing social and environmental sustainability. Here are five ways impact investing can contribute to SDG 8:

Firstly, impact investors can invest in social enterprises that aim to create positive social and environmental impact while generating financial returns. This can help create new jobs and promote sustainable economic growth.

Secondly, impact investors can invest in companies and projects that promote fair labor practices, such as living wages, safe working conditions, and workers' rights. This can help reduce labor exploitation and promote social justice.

Thirdly, impact investors can invest in companies and projects that address income inequality, such as affordable housing, education, and healthcare. This can help reduce poverty and promote economic mobility.

Fourthly, impact investors can invest in companies and projects that promote sustainable supply chains, such as fair trade, organic farming, and responsible mining. This can help reduce environmental degradation and promote social responsibility.

Lastly, impact investors can invest in companies and projects that promote economic development in underserved communities, such as rural areas, indigenous communities, and low-income neighborhoods. This can help reduce economic disparities and promote social inclusion.

In conclusion, impact investing can contribute significantly to SDG 8 by promoting social and environmental sustainability, fair labor practices, income equality, sustainable supply chains, and economic development in underserved communities. By investing in these areas, impact investors can help create decent work and economic growth, reduce poverty and promote sustainable development.

SDG 9: Industry, Innovation, and Infrastructure

Industry, innovation, and infrastructure are critical to promoting sustainable development and economic growth. Impact investors can drive innovation and infrastructure development by investing in companies and projects promoting social and environmental sustainability. Here are five ways impact investing can contribute to SDG 9:

Firstly, impact investors can invest in companies and projects that build and maintain sustainable infrastructure, such as renewable energy, public transit, and green buildings. This can help reduce environmental impact and promote social and economic sustainability.

Secondly, impact investors can invest in companies and projects promoting sustainability innovation, such as clean technology, circular economy, and sustainable agriculture. This can help drive economic growth and environmental sustainability.

Thirdly, impact investors can invest in companies and projects that address the digital divide, such as broadband access, digital literacy, and e-commerce. This can help reduce economic disparities and promote social inclusion.

Fourthly, impact investors can invest in companies and projects that promote sustainable tourism, such as eco-tourism, cultural tourism, and community-based tourism. This can help promote economic development and environmental conservation.

Lastly, impact investors can invest in companies and projects that promote infrastructure development in underserved communities, such as rural areas, indigenous communities, and low-income neighborhoods. This can help reduce economic disparities and promote social inclusion.

Impact investors can help drive sustainable development and economic growth by investing in these areas while promoting social and environmental sustainability.

Impact investing can play a critical role in achieving Sustainable Development Goals. By investing in companies and projects that promote social and environmental sustainability, impact investors can drive positive change while generating financial returns. This chapter explored how impact investing can contribute to SDGs 5-9, which is critical for creating a more equitable, sustainable, and prosperous world.

Chapter Summary

- Impact investing can promote gender equality by investing in women-led businesses, supporting women's health and well-being, promoting gender diversity and inclusion, addressing gender-based violence, and supporting women's economic empowerment.

- Impact investing can address the global water crisis by investing in water infrastructure, supporting water conservation, addressing water pollution, providing access to sanitation, and supporting water-related entrepreneurship.
- Impact investing can accelerate the transition to a low-carbon economy by investing in renewable energy, supporting energy efficiency, addressing energy poverty, promoting sustainable transportation, and supporting energy-related entrepreneurship.
- Impact investing can create decent work and economic growth by investing in social enterprises, supporting fair labor practices, addressing income inequality, promoting sustainable supply chains, and supporting economic development in underserved communities.
- Impact investing can drive innovation and infrastructure development by investing in sustainable infrastructure, supporting innovation for sustainability, addressing the digital divide, promoting sustainable tourism, and supporting infrastructure development in underserved communities.

7

IMPACT INVESTING AND SUSTAINABLE DEVELOPMENT GOALS (CONT.)

A city skyline, with buildings made from sustainable materials and powered by renewable energy, illustrating the transformative impact of impact investing on urban development and climate action.

Impact investing is a powerful tool that can help achieve the Sustainable Development Goals (SDGs) set by the United Nations. The previous chapter discussed SDGs 5-9 and how to impact investing can contribute to their achievement. This chapter will explore SDGs 10-14 and how to impact investing can help reduce inequalities, create sustainable cities and communities, promote responsible consumption and production, take climate action, and protect life below water. By investing in companies and projects that align with these goals, impact investors can positively impact the world while generating financial returns.

SDG 10: Reduced Inequalities

SDG 10 aims to reduce inequalities within and among countries. This includes reducing income inequality, promoting social, economic, and political inclusion, and ensuring equal opportunities for all. Impact investors can contribute to this goal by investing in companies that promote diversity and inclusion, provide access to education and healthcare, and create job opportunities for marginalized communities. For example, impact investors can invest in microfinance institutions that provide loans to women entrepreneurs or companies that provide affordable housing for low-income families.

Investing in companies that promote diversity and inclusion can also lead to better financial performance. Studies have shown that companies with diverse leadership teams and inclusive cultures outperform their peers. By investing in these companies, impact investors can positively impact society and generate financial returns.

However, impact investors must also be aware of the potential risks of investing in companies that claim to promote diversity and inclusion but do not follow through on their promises. Therefore, it is important to conduct thorough due diligence and ensure that the companies align with the investor's values and goals.

In addition to investing in companies, impact investors can support organizations that advocate for policies promoting equality and inclusion. Using their influence and resources, impact investors can help create a more just and equitable society.

SDG 11: Sustainable Cities and Communities

SDG 11 aims to make cities and human settlements inclusive, safe, resilient, and sustainable. This includes promoting sustainable transportation, reducing air pollution, providing access to affordable housing, and protecting cultural and natural heritage. Impact investors can contribute to this goal by investing in companies that develop sustainable infrastructure, promote renewable energy, and provide affordable housing.

For example, impact investors can invest in companies that develop sustainable transportation solutions such as electric vehicles or public transportation systems. They can also invest in companies that promote renewable energy, such as solar or wind power. As a result, impact investors can help reduce carbon emissions and promote a more sustainable future by investing in these companies.

Investing in affordable housing is also important to promote sustainable cities and communities. For example, impact investors can invest in companies that provide affordable housing for low-income families or organizations that advocate for policies promoting affordable housing. By doing so, impact investors can help reduce homelessness and improve the quality of life for millions of people.

SDG 12: Responsible Consumption and Production

SDG 12 aims to ensure sustainable consumption and production patterns. This includes promoting resource efficiency, reducing waste, and promoting sustainable lifestyles. Impact investors can contribute to this goal by investing in companies that promote sustainable production methods, reduce waste, and develop sustainable products.

For example, impact investors can invest in companies that develop sustainable packaging solutions or in companies that promote circular economy models. They can also invest in companies that develop sustainable agriculture practices or promote sustainable fishing practices. By investing in these companies, impact investors can help reduce waste and promote sustainable consumption and production patterns.

Impact investors can also support organizations that promote sustainable lifestyles and educate consumers about the impact of their choices. By doing so, impact investors can help create a more sustainable future.

SDG 13: Climate Action

SDG 13 aims to take urgent action to combat climate change and its impacts. This includes reducing greenhouse gas emissions, promoting renewable energy, and increasing climate resilience. Impact investors can contribute to this goal by investing in companies that develop renewable energy solutions, promote energy efficiency, and reduce carbon emissions.

For example, impact investors can invest in companies that develop solar or wind power solutions or in companies that promote energy-efficient buildings. They can also invest in companies that develop carbon capture and storage technologies or in companies that promote sustainable transportation solutions. As a result, impact investors can help reduce carbon emissions and promote a more sustainable future by investing in these companies.

Impact investors can also support organizations advocating for climate action policies. Using their influence and resources, impact investors can help create a more sustainable future for all.

SDG 14: Life Below Water

SDG 14 aims to conserve and sustainably use the oceans, seas, and marine resources for sustainable development. This includes reducing marine pollution, protecting marine ecosystems, and promoting sustainable fishing practices. Impact investors can contribute to this goal by investing in companies that promote sustainable fishing practices, reduce marine pollution, and protect marine ecosystems.

For example, impact investors can invest in companies that develop sustainable aquaculture practices or promote sustainable fishing practices. They can also invest in companies that develop technologies to reduce marine pollution or in organizations that advocate for policies that protect marine ecosystems. By investing in these companies, impact investors can help promote sustainable development and protect life below water.

Impact investing can play a crucial role in achieving Sustainable Development Goals. By investing in companies and projects that align with these goals, impact investors can positively impact the world while generating financial returns. This chapter explored how to impact investing can contribute to SDG 10: Reduced Inequalities, SDG 11: Sustainable Cities and Communities, SDG 12: Responsible Consumption and Production, SDG 13: Climate Action, and SDG 14: Life Below Water. Impact investors can help create a more just, equitable, and sustainable world by investing in these areas.

Chapter Summary

- Impact investors can contribute to SDG 10 by investing in companies that promote diversity and inclusion and provide access to education and healthcare.
- Investing in companies promoting diversity and inclusion can improve financial performance.
- Impact investors can support organizations that advocate for policies that promote equality and inclusion.
- Impact investors can contribute to SDG 11 by investing in companies that develop sustainable infrastructure and promote renewable energy.
- Investing in affordable housing is important to promote sustainable cities and communities.

- Impact investors can contribute to SDG 12 by investing in companies that promote sustainable production methods and reduce waste.
- Impact investors can support organizations that promote sustainable lifestyles and educate consumers about the impact of their choices.
- Impact investors can contribute to SDG 13 by investing in companies that develop renewable energy solutions and promote energy efficiency.

8

IMPACT INVESTING AND SUSTAINABLE DEVELOPMENT GOALS (CONT.)

A lightbulb surrounded by a green environment, representing the innovative and sustainable solutions that impact investing can generate to address pressing social and environmental challenges, such as climate change and biodiversity loss.

Impact investing has emerged as a powerful tool to address the world's most pressing social and environmental challenges. It is a form of investing that seeks to generate measurable social and environmental impact alongside financial returns. This chapter will explore the relationship between impact investing and the Sustainable Development Goals (SDGs), a set of 17 global goals adopted by the United Nations in 2015 to end poverty, protect the planet, and ensure prosperity for all. We will examine how impact investing can contribute to achieving the three remaining SDGs: Life on Land (SDG 15), Peace, Justice and Strong Institutions (SDG 16), and Partnerships for the Goals (SDG 17). We will also discuss the future of sustainable development and the role of governments in promoting impact investing.

SDG 15: Life on Land

SDG 15 aims to protect, restore, and promote the sustainable use of terrestrial ecosystems, sustainably manage forests, combat desertification, and halt and reverse land degradation and biodiversity loss. Impact investing can be crucial in achieving this goal by providing capital to businesses and organizations working to conserve and restore ecosystems, promote sustainable agriculture, and protect biodiversity.

One example of impact investing in SDG 15 is the Rainforest Alliance's certification program, which helps farmers and forest managers adopt sustainable practices that protect ecosystems and improve livelihoods. Impact investors can support this program by investing in companies that produce sustainably produced commodities like coffee, cocoa, and timber. Another example is the Wildlife Conservation Society's Conservation Solutions Fund, which provides grants and loans to conservation entrepreneurs developing innovative solutions to protect wildlife and ecosystems.

Impact investing in SDG 15 can also help address the root causes of deforestation and land degradation, such as poverty and lack of access to finance. In addition, by investing in businesses that provide sustainable livelihoods to local communities, impact investors can help reduce the pressure on forests and other natural resources. For example, Root Capital provides loans and training to small and growing businesses in rural areas, helping them to improve their productivity and sustainability.

In addition to providing capital, impact investors can promote policy and regulatory frameworks supporting sustainable land use. By engaging with governments and other stakeholders, impact investors can advocate for policies that incentivize sustainable practices and discourage destructive activities. For example, the Global Impact Investing Network's Land Use Working Group is working to develop a set of principles for responsible land use investment.

Overall, impact investing can be a powerful tool for achieving SDG 15 by providing capital, promoting sustainable practices, and advocating for policy change.

SDG 16: Peace, Justice, and Strong Institutions

SDG 16 aims to promote peaceful and inclusive societies, provide access to justice for all, and build effective, accountable, and inclusive institutions at all levels. Impact investing can contribute to achieving this goal by supporting businesses and organizations that promote social justice, human rights, and good governance.

One example of impact investing in SDG 16 is the International Finance Corporation's (IFC) Access to Justice program, which provides financing and technical assistance to legal service providers in developing countries. By improving access to justice for marginalized communities, this program helps to promote social justice and human rights. Another example is the Omidyar Network's Governance & Citizen Engagement initiative, which supports organizations that promote transparency, accountability, and citizen participation in government.

Impact investing in SDG 16 can also help build strong and inclusive institutions by providing capital to businesses that promote economic development and job creation. By supporting small and medium-sized enterprises (SMEs) in developing countries, impact investors can help to build a more inclusive economy and reduce poverty. For example, the African Development Bank's SME Program provides financing and technical assistance to African SMEs, helping them grow and create jobs.

In addition to providing capital, impact investors can promote good governance and accountability. By engaging with governments and other stakeholders, impact investors can advocate for policies that promote transparency, reduce corruption, and strengthen institutions. For example, the Principles for Responsible Investment's (PRI) Engagements on Governance program engages with companies and governments to promote good governance practices.

Overall, impact investing can be a powerful tool for achieving SDG 16 by supporting businesses promoting social justice, human rights, and good governance and advocating for policy change.

SDG 17: Partnerships for the Goals

SDG 17 aims to strengthen the means of implementation and revitalize the global partnership for sustainable development. Impact investing can contribute to achieving this goal by fostering partnerships between investors, businesses, governments, and civil society organizations.

One example of impact investing in SDG 17 is the Global Impact Investing Network's (GIIN) ImpactBase platform. It connects impact investors with investment opportunities that align with their social and environmental goals. By providing a marketplace for impact investments, ImpactBase helps to facilitate partnerships between investors and businesses. Another example is the IFC's Scaling Solar program, which helps governments in developing countries to attract private sector investment in solar energy projects. By bringing together governments, investors, and project developers, this program helps to create partnerships that promote sustainable development.

Impact investing in SDG 17 can also help to build capacity and promote knowledge sharing among stakeholders. By investing in education and training programs, impact investors can build the skills and knowledge needed to promote sustainable development. For example, the Acumen Fund's Lean Data initiative provides training and tools to help social enterprises measure their impact and improve performance.

In addition to fostering partnerships, impact investors can also play a role in promoting innovation and entrepreneurship. By investing in businesses developing innovative solutions to social and environmental challenges, impact investors can help drive progress toward the SDGs. For example, the Unreasonable Group's Unreasonable Impact program supports high-growth companies addressing social and environmental challenges, providing them mentorship, resources, and access to capital.

Overall, impact investing can be a powerful tool for achieving SDG 17 by fostering partnerships, building capacity, promoting innovation, and driving progress toward the SDGs.

Impact Investing and the Future of Sustainable Development

Impact investing can play a significant role in achieving the SDGs and promoting sustainable development more broadly. However, realizing this potential will require continued growth and innovation in the impact investing industry.

One key challenge facing impact investing is the need for more **standardized impact measurement and reporting.** With clear and consistent metrics for measuring social and environmental impact, it can be easier for investors to assess the effectiveness of their investments. The Impact Management Project, a collaborative effort by leading impact investing organizations, is working to develop a set of standardized impact metrics and reporting practices.

Another challenge is the need for more capital to flow into impact investing. While the impact investing industry has grown significantly in recent years, it still represents a small fraction of the overall investment market. To attract more capital, impact investors must demonstrate that they can generate competitive financial returns alongside measurable social and environmental impact.

Finally, impact investing must continue evolving and adapting to social and environmental challenges. As new issues emerge, impact investors must develop new investment strategies and approaches to addressing them. For example, the COVID-19 pandemic has highlighted the need for healthcare, education, and social safety net investments.

Overall, the future of sustainable development will depend in part on the growth and evolution of impact investing. By addressing these challenges and continuing to innovate, impact investors can help to drive progress towards a more sustainable and equitable world.

Impact Investing and the Role of Governments

Governments have a critical role in promoting impact investing and achieving the SDGs. By creating supportive policy and regulatory frameworks, governments can help to unlock private sector capital and promote sustainable development.

One key policy tool for promoting impact investing is **tax incentives.** Governments can encourage more capital to flow into the impact investing industry by providing tax breaks for impact investments. For example, the UK government's Social Investment Tax Relief program provides tax breaks for investments in social enterprises.

Another important policy tool is public-private partnerships. Governments can leverage private sector expertise and resources to achieve social and environmental goals by partnering with the private sector. For example, the US government's Power Africa initiative is a public-private partnership that aims to increase access to electricity in sub-Saharan Africa by mobilizing private sector investment.

In addition to creating supportive policy frameworks, governments can promote impact investing through their investments. By investing in impact funds and supporting impact-oriented businesses, governments can demonstrate the viability and potential of impact investing. For example, the French government's Bpifrance invests in impact funds and provides financing to impact-oriented businesses.

Overall, governments are critical in promoting impact investing and achieving the SDGs. By creating supportive policy frameworks, partnering with the private sector, and investing in impact-oriented businesses, governments can help to unlock private sector capital and drive progress towards a more sustainable and equitable world.

Chapter Summary

- Impact investing can contribute to achieving SDG 15 by providing capital, promoting sustainable practices, and advocating for policy change.
- Impact investing can contribute to achieving SDG 16 by supporting businesses that promote social justice, human rights, and good governance and advocating for policy change.
- Impact investing can contribute to achieving SDG 17 by fostering partnerships, building capacity, promoting innovation, and driving progress toward the SDGs.
- The future of sustainable development will depend in part on the growth and evolution of impact investing, including the development of standardized impact metrics, the attraction of more capital, and the adaptation to new challenges.
- Governments are critical in promoting impact investing and achieving the SDGs through tax incentives, public-private partnerships, and investments in impact-oriented businesses.

9

IMPACT INVESTING AND SOCIAL ENTREPRENEURSHIP

A vibrant city street, with storefronts that showcase different impact investing initiatives, from sustainable fashion boutiques to eco-friendly cafes and community gardens.

Social entrepreneurship and impact investing are two concepts that have gained significant attention in recent years. They aim to create positive social and environmental impact while generating financial returns. In this chapter, we will explore the definition of social entrepreneurship, its relationship with impact investing, different social entrepreneurship models, the role of innovation in social entrepreneurship, and the importance of sustainability.

Definition of Social Entrepreneurship

Social entrepreneurship is a dynamic and multifaceted concept that has gained significant traction recently. It is a term that refers to the practice of creating innovative solutions to social and environmental problems. Social entrepreneurs use their creativity, passion, and business acumen to address social and environmental challenges. They are driven by a desire to create positive change and improve the lives of people and communities.

Social entrepreneurship is not limited to any particular sector or industry. It can take many forms, including nonprofits, for-profits, and hybrid organizations. Social entrepreneurs are found in various fields, including healthcare, education, energy, and agriculture. They are united by their commitment to creating sustainable solutions that can be scaled and replicated to address systemic social and environmental challenges.

One of the key differences between social entrepreneurship and traditional entrepreneurship is the prioritization of social and environmental impact over financial returns. While traditional entrepreneurs primarily focus on generating profits, social entrepreneurs measure success by the bottom line and the positive impact they create. In addition, they are committed to creating sustainable solutions that can be scaled and replicated to address systemic social and environmental challenges.

Social entrepreneurship is a powerful force for positive change in the world. It has the potential to transform the way we think about business and the role it can play in creating a better world. Social entrepreneurs are creating a more just, equitable, and sustainable future for all by harnessing the power of innovation, creativity, and business acumen.

Social Entrepreneurship and Impact Investing

Social entrepreneurship and impact investing are two concepts that have gained significant traction in recent years. Both focus on creating positive social and environmental impact but approach this goal differently. Social entrepreneurship is using business principles to solve social and environmental problems. Impact investing, on the other hand, is a form of investing that seeks to generate social and environmental impact alongside financial returns.

Impact investors are individuals or organizations that invest in social enterprises, nonprofits, and other organizations committed to creating positive social and environmental impact. Unlike traditional investors, impact investors prioritize impact over financial returns. As a result, they accept lower financial returns in exchange for knowing that their investments make a positive difference.

Social entrepreneurs often rely on impact investors to fund their ventures. These investors provide social entrepreneurs the capital they need to scale their solutions and create greater impact. Impact investors also provide social entrepreneurs the expertise and resources they need to succeed. In addition, they may offer guidance on business strategy, marketing, and other key areas, as well as connections to other investors and potential partners.

One of the key benefits of impact investing is that it allows investors to **align their investments with their values**. In addition, by investing in organizations that are working to create positive social and environmental impact, impact investors can feel good about the impact their money is making. This can especially appeal to younger investors looking to make a positive difference.

Social entrepreneurship and impact investing are powerful tools for creating positive social and environmental impact. Social entrepreneurs and impact investors can create innovative solutions to some of the world's most pressing problems by working together. Whether it's addressing climate change, reducing poverty, or improving access to healthcare, social entrepreneurship, and impact investing have the potential to make a real difference in the world.

Social Entrepreneurship Models

Social entrepreneurship is a rapidly growing field that seeks to address social and environmental issues through innovative business models. There are several different social entrepreneurship models, each with strengths and weaknesses. These models include nonprofits, for-profits, and hybrid organizations.

Nonprofits are organizations dedicated to a social or environmental mission and do not distribute profits to shareholders. As a result, they are often better suited for addressing immediate social and environmental needs, such as providing food and shelter to those in need or responding to natural disasters. Instead, nonprofits rely on donations and grants to fund their operations. As a result, their impact on their target population often measures their success.

On the other hand, for-profits aim to generate financial returns while also creating social and environmental impact. As a result, they are often better suited for creating sustainable solutions that can be scaled and replicated, such as developing new technologies or business models that address social and environmental issues. For-profits rely on revenue from their products or services to fund their operations. Their success is often measured by their financial performance and social and environmental impact.

Hybrid organizations combine elements of both nonprofits and for-profits. They seek to create social and environmental impact while generating financial returns and often have a dual bottom line. Hybrid organizations can take many forms, such as social enterprises, benefit corporations, or community interest companies. They face unique challenges in balancing their social and financial goals. Their success is often measured by their ability to achieve both.

Overall, social entrepreneurship models offer a range of options for addressing social and environmental issues. Each model has its strengths and weaknesses, and the choice of model will depend on the specific goals and needs of the organization. Nevertheless, by leveraging the power of business to create positive social and environmental impact, social entrepreneurship can transform how we address some of the world's most pressing challenges.

Social Entrepreneurship and Innovation

Social entrepreneurship is a rapidly growing field that combines business principles with social and environmental goals. It allows individuals and organizations to create positive change in the world while generating revenue and creating sustainable solutions. One of the key components of social entrepreneurship is innovation, which is used to create new solutions to complex social and environmental challenges.

Innovation is essential for social entrepreneurs because it allows them to constantly experiment and iterate until they find the most effective and sustainable solutions. This process can take many forms, including developing new technologies, business models, and partnerships. As a result, social entrepreneurs can create more efficient, effective, and impactful solutions by embracing innovation.

In addition to creating new solutions, social entrepreneurs also use innovation to develop new funding models. For example, crowdfunding, impact investing, and social impact bonds are all innovative funding models that have emerged in recent years. These models provide social entrepreneurs with new sources of capital and allow them to scale their solutions more quickly.

Crowdfunding is a popular funding model that allows social entrepreneurs to raise money from many people through online platforms. This model is particularly effective for projects with a strong social or environmental mission, as it allows individuals to contribute small amounts of money to support a cause they believe in.

Impact investing is another innovative funding model that has recently gained popularity. This model involves investing in companies or organizations with a social or environmental mission to generate financial returns and positive social impact. Impact investors are looking for companies that are creating positive change in the world and are willing to invest in them to help them grow and scale their impact.

Social impact bonds are a more complex funding model that involves private investors providing upfront capital to fund social programs. If the program successfully achieves its goals, the investors receive a return on their investment. This model is particularly effective for programs with a measurable impact, as it allows investors to see a direct return on their investment.

Overall, innovation is a critical component of social entrepreneurship. Social entrepreneurs can create more effective and sustainable solutions to complex social and environmental challenges by embracing new technologies, business models, and funding models. As the field of social entrepreneurship continues to grow, we will see even more innovative solutions emerge in the years to come.

Social Entrepreneurship and Sustainability

Social entrepreneurship is a rapidly growing field gaining recognition for its ability to create innovative solutions to some of the world's most pressing social and environmental challenges. One of the key components of social entrepreneurship is sustainability, which refers to the ability of a solution to be maintained over the long term.

Sustainability is a multifaceted concept encompassing environmental, social, and financial sustainability. Social entrepreneurs recognize that their solutions must be environmentally sustainable to minimize their impact on the planet and ensure that future generations can continue to benefit from them. This means they must consider the entire lifecycle of their products or services, from production to disposal, and strive to minimize waste and pollution at every stage.

In addition to environmental sustainability, social entrepreneurs also prioritize social sustainability. This means their solutions must be designed to create a positive social impact over the long term. They must consider the needs and perspectives of all stakeholders, including the communities they serve, and work to build relationships based on trust and mutual respect. Social entrepreneurs must also ensure their solutions are culturally appropriate and sensitive to local customs and traditions.

Finally, social entrepreneurs must ensure that their solutions are financially sustainable. This means that they must be able to generate the revenue they need to sustain their operations over the long term. Therefore, they must develop business models that are financially viable, scalable, and adapt to changing market conditions. Social entrepreneurs must also be able to measure and communicate their solutions' social and environmental impact to attract funding and support from investors and other stakeholders.

In summary, sustainability is a critical component of social entrepreneurship. Social entrepreneurs must create environmentally, socially, and financially sustainable solutions to address systemic social and environmental challenges. Social entrepreneurs can create lasting impact by prioritizing sustainability and contributing to a more equitable and sustainable world.

Social entrepreneurship and impact investing are powerful tools for creating positive social and environmental impact. They desire to create sustainable solutions that can be scaled and replicated to address systemic social and environmental challenges. Social entrepreneurship and impact investing are not just about generating financial returns; they are about creating a better world for all.

Chapter Summary

- Social entrepreneurship is creating innovative solutions to social and environmental problems.
- Impact investing seeks to generate social and environmental impact alongside financial returns.

- Several social entrepreneurship models exist, including nonprofits, for-profits, and hybrid organizations.
- Innovation is a critical component of social entrepreneurship.
- Sustainability is another critical component of social entrepreneurship.
- Social entrepreneurs aim to create environmentally, socially, and financially sustainable solutions.
- Social entrepreneurs must ensure that their solutions are financially viable and can generate the revenue they need to sustain their operations.
- Social entrepreneurs must also ensure that their solutions are socially sustainable and can create a positive social impact over the long term.

10

IMPACT INVESTING AND CORPORATE SOCIAL RESPONSIBILITY

A tree with roots made of coins and leaves made of hearts, symbolizing the positive impact of impact investing and corporate social responsibility on the environment and society.

In today's world, businesses are about more than just making profits. They are also expected to contribute to society and the environment. This is where Corporate Social Responsibility (CSR) comes into play. CSR is a concept that has gained immense popularity in recent years. It refers to the responsibility of businesses towards society and the environment. Impact investing, on the other hand, is a relatively new concept that aims to generate social and environmental impact along with financial returns. This chapter will explore the relationship between CSR and impact investing and how they can work together to create a better world.

Definition of Corporate Social Responsibility

Corporate Social Responsibility (CSR) is a concept that refers to the responsibility of businesses toward society and the environment. Businesses take a voluntary initiative to go beyond their legal obligations and contribute to society. CSR involves considering business operations' social, environmental, and economic impacts and making decisions that benefit all stakeholders, including employees, customers, suppliers, communities, and the environment.

CSR is **not just about philanthropy or charity**. We are integrating social and environmental considerations into business operations and decision-making processes. As a result, CSR can help businesses build a positive reputation, attract and retain customers and employees, and create long-term value for all stakeholders.

Corporate Social Responsibility and Impact Investing

Corporate Social Responsibility (CSR) and Impact Investing are two concepts that have gained significant attention in recent years. CSR refers to the responsibility that businesses have towards society and the environment. It involves taking actions that benefit society and the environment beyond the legal requirements. Impact investing, on the other hand, is a relatively new concept that aims to generate social and environmental impact and financial returns.

Impact investors invest in businesses that have a positive social or environmental impact. These businesses are often referred to as social enterprises or impact-driven businesses. Impact investing can be seen as a form of CSR, as it involves businesses taking responsibility for their impact on society and the environment.

The concept of shared value is central to both CSR and impact investing. Shared value refers to the idea that businesses can create value for themselves and society at the same time. By investing in businesses that have a positive impact, impact investors can help create a better world while also generating financial returns.

Impact investing has gained significant momentum in recent years, with more and more investors looking to invest in businesses with a positive impact. This has led to the growth of impact-driven businesses and the development of new financial instruments, such as social impact bonds and green bonds.

In conclusion, CSR and impact investing are two concepts that are closely related. Both involve businesses taking responsibility for their impact on society and the environment. Impact investing can help businesses create shared value, where financial, social, and environmental value is created. By investing in businesses that have a positive impact, impact investors can help create a better world while also generating financial returns.

Corporate Social Responsibility Models

Corporate Social Responsibility (CSR) is a concept that has gained significant attention in recent years. It refers to the responsibility of businesses to operate in a manner that benefits society and the environment in addition to generating profits. Businesses can adopt several CSR models, each with its unique approach to achieving this goal.

The **philanthropic model** is one of the most common CSR models. It involves businesses donating money or resources to charitable causes. Businesses often use this model to give back to the community and improve their public image. By supporting charitable causes, businesses can demonstrate their commitment to social responsibility and build goodwill with their customers and stakeholders.

Another popular CSR model is the **stakeholder model.** This model involves businesses considering the interests of all stakeholders, including employees, customers, suppliers, communities, and the environment. The stakeholder model recognizes that businesses are responsible for balancing the needs of all stakeholders, not just shareholders. By taking a stakeholder approach, businesses can build stronger relationships with their stakeholders, improve their reputation, and create a more sustainable business model.

The shared value model is a relatively new CSR model that recently gained popularity. This model involves businesses creating value for themselves, society, and the environment. The shared value model recognizes that businesses can create economic value by addressing social and environmental challenges. By creating shared value, businesses can improve their competitiveness while contributing to the greater good.

In conclusion, businesses can adopt several CSR models, each with its unique approach to achieving social responsibility. For example, the philanthropic model involves businesses donating money or resources to charitable causes. In contrast, the stakeholder model involves businesses considering the interests of all stakeholders. Finally, the shared value model involves businesses creating value for themselves, society, and the environment. By adopting these models, businesses can demonstrate their commitment to social responsibility, build stronger relationships with their stakeholders, and create a more sustainable business model.

Corporate Social Responsibility and Innovation

Corporate Social Responsibility (CSR) is a concept that has gained significant attention in recent years. It refers to the responsibility of businesses to operate in a manner that is ethical, sustainable, and beneficial to society. CSR involves considering the impact of business operations on the environment, employees, customers, and the wider community. One way that businesses can demonstrate their commitment to CSR is through innovation.

Innovation is creating new ideas, products, or services that add value to society. It involves taking risks, experimenting with new approaches, and challenging the status quo. Innovation can play a crucial role in CSR by enabling businesses to create products or services with a positive social or environmental impact. For example, a company might develop a new technology that reduces carbon emissions or a product made from sustainable materials.

Innovation can also help businesses to reduce their environmental footprint or improve the working conditions of their employees. For example, a company might develop a new manufacturing process that uses less energy or a new system for tracking employee health and safety. By investing in innovation. As a result, businesses can improve their operations and demonstrate their commitment to CSR.

Moreover, innovation can help businesses to create new markets or opportunities. By addressing social or environmental challenges, businesses can tap into new markets or create new products or services that meet the needs of consumers. For example, a company might develop a new product to address a specific social or environmental issue, such as reducing plastic waste or improving access to clean water.

In conclusion, innovation and CSR are closely linked. By investing in innovation, businesses can create products or services with a positive social or environmental impact, reduce their environmental footprint, improve working conditions, and create new markets or opportunities. As such, businesses prioritizing innovation as part of their CSR strategy will likely be more successful in the long run.

Corporate Social Responsibility and Sustainability

Corporate Social Responsibility (CSR) and Sustainability are two intertwined concepts that have become increasingly important in business. Sustainability, in particular, has become a key aspect of CSR as businesses are now expected to take responsibility for their impact on the environment and society.

In today's world, businesses are expected not only to generate profits but also to operate sustainably. This means that they must ensure that their operations do not harm the environment and take steps to reduce their carbon footprint. This involves adopting sustainable practices such as using renewable energy sources, reducing waste, and conserving natural resources.

Sustainability is not just about being environmentally friendly; it also has economic and social benefits. By adopting sustainable practices, businesses can reduce costs, improve their reputation, and attract and retain customers and employees. For example, businesses that use renewable energy sources can reduce their energy bills. In contrast, those that reduce waste can save on disposal costs.

Moreover, sustainability can help businesses create long-term value. By investing in sustainable practices, businesses can future-proof their operations and ensure longevity. In addition, sustainable practices are often more efficient and cost-effective in the long run. Finally, they can help businesses adapt to changing market conditions.

In conclusion, sustainability is a crucial aspect of CSR. Businesses must take responsibility for their impact on the environment and society. By adopting sustainable practices, businesses can reduce their environmental footprint, create long-term value, and improve their reputation.

CSR and impact investing are two concepts that can work together to create a better world. Businesses can create shared value and generate positive social and environmental impact and financial returns by taking responsibility for their impact on society and the environment. In addition, by adopting sustainable practices and innovating, businesses can create long-term value and contribute to a more sustainable future.

Chapter Summary

- CSR refers to the responsibility of businesses towards society and the environment.
- Impact investing aims to generate social and environmental impact and financial returns.
- CSR and impact investing can work together to create shared value.
- The philanthropic, stakeholder, and shared value models are common models of CSR.
- Innovation can play a crucial role in CSR.
- Sustainability is a key aspect of CSR.
- Adopting sustainable practices can help businesses create long-term value.
- CSR and impact investing can contribute to a more sustainable and equitable future.

11

IMPACT INVESTING AND ETHICAL INVESTING

A ripple effect spreading out from a single drop in a pond, representing the positive impact that impact investing and corporate social responsibility can have on society and the world as a whole.

As the world becomes more aware of the impact of businesses on society and the environment, ethical investing has become a popular way for investors to align their values with their financial goals. Impact investing takes this a step further by actively seeking out investments that positively impact society and the environment. This chapter will explore the definitions of ethical and impact investing, the different models of ethical investing, and how ethical investing can drive innovation and sustainability.

Definition of Ethical Investing

Ethical investing, also known as socially responsible investing (SRI), is investing in companies that align with an investor's values and beliefs. This can include avoiding companies that engage in activities such as tobacco, weapons, or fossil fuels or investing in companies that prioritize diversity, human rights, and environmental sustainability. Ethical investing can also involve engaging with companies to encourage them to adopt more responsible practices.

Ethical investing has become increasingly popular in recent years, with more investors looking to align their investments with their values. According to a Global Sustainable Investment Alliance report, sustainable investing assets reached $30.7 trillion in 2018, a 34% increase from 2016.

Ethical Investing and Impact Investing

In today's world, investing is not just about making money but also about making a difference. Ethical investing and impact investing are two approaches that have gained popularity in recent years. While both aim to align investments with personal values, their approach, and objectives differ.

Ethical investing is a strategy that focuses on avoiding harm by investing in companies that meet certain ethical standards. This may include avoiding investments in companies that engage in activities such as tobacco, weapons, or animal testing. In addition, ethical investors seek to align their investments with their values and beliefs, often prioritizing social responsibility over financial returns.

On the other hand, impact investing seeks to actively create positive change by investing in companies, organizations, and funds with a measurable social or environmental impact. Impact investors aim to generate financial returns while positively impacting issues such as climate change, poverty, and inequality. They seek to use their investments as a tool for social and environmental change.

The impact investing market has grown significantly in recent years, with many investors looking to make a positive impact with their investments. According to the Global Impact Investing Network, analysts estimated the size of the impact investing market to be $715 billion in 2020. This growth is driven by a growing awareness of the need for sustainable and socially responsible investments and a desire to positively impact the world.

In conclusion, ethical investing and impact investing are two approaches that aim to align investments with personal values and beliefs. While ethical investing focuses on avoiding harm, impact investing seeks to create positive change actively. As the impact investing market continues to grow, investors have the opportunity to make a positive impact on the world while also generating financial returns.

Ethical Investing Models

Ethical investing has become increasingly popular as investors seek to align their financial goals with their values. Investors can choose from several models of ethical investing, each with its unique approach to promoting responsible investment practices.

One of the most common models of ethical investing is **negative screening.** This approach involves avoiding investments in companies that engage in harmful or unethical activities. For example, investors may avoid investing in companies that produce tobacco products and weapons or engage in environmentally damaging practices.

On the other hand, positive screening involves actively seeking out investments in companies that prioritize environmental, social, and governance (ESG) factors. This approach identifies companies committed to sustainable business practices, such as reducing their carbon footprint, promoting diversity and inclusion, and prioritizing employee well-being.

Another model of ethical investing is shareholder advocacy. This approach involves engaging with companies to encourage them to adopt more responsible practices. For example, shareholders may use their voting power to push for company policy or practice changes. In addition, they may engage in dialogue with company management to encourage them to take action on issues such as climate change, human rights, or social justice.

Overall, ethical investing models offer investors a range of options for aligning their investments with their values. For example, investing in companies prioritizing ESG factors or engaging in shareholder advocacy can help promote positive change and contribute to a more sustainable and responsible global economy.

Ethical Investing and Innovation

Ethical investing has become an increasingly popular trend in recent years as more and more investors seek to align their financial goals with their values. This approach to investing involves selecting companies that prioritize environmental, social, and governance (ESG) factors, such as sustainability, diversity, and transparency. By investing in these companies, investors can earn a return on their investment and support businesses that positively impact society and the environment.

One of the key benefits of ethical investing is that it can drive innovation by encouraging companies to adopt more sustainable and responsible practices. When investors demand that companies prioritize ESG factors, it creates a market for sustainable products and services. This, in turn, can lead to increased innovation in areas such as renewable energy, sustainable agriculture, and green transportation.

For example, companies prioritizing sustainability may invest in research and development to create more efficient and eco-friendly products. This could include developing new solar power, wind energy, or electric vehicle technologies. Investing in these companies can support these innovations and contribute to a more sustainable future.

Furthermore, ethical investing can positively impact society by promoting social responsibility and diversity. Companies prioritizing ESG factors are likelier to have diverse leadership teams and inclusive workplace cultures. This can lead to better decision-making, improved employee morale, and a stronger commitment to social responsibility.

In conclusion, ethical investing is a way to align your financial goals with your values and drive innovation and promote positive social and environmental change. Investing in companies prioritizing ESG factors can help create a market for sustainable products and services, support innovative companies, and contribute to a more sustainable and equitable future.

Ethical Investing and Sustainability

Ethical investing is a concept that has gained significant traction in recent years as more and more investors are looking to align their investments with their values. At its core, ethical investing is about investing in companies that prioritize sustainability and social responsibility while avoiding those that engage in harmful practices to the environment or society.

One of the key benefits of ethical investing is its **potential to promote sustainability**. Investing in companies prioritizing sustainability can help create a market for sustainable products and services. This, in turn, can lead to increased adoption of sustainable practices and technologies, which can help mitigate the impacts of climate change and promote a more sustainable future.

Moreover, ethical investing can also encourage companies to adopt more responsible practices. When investors choose to invest in companies that prioritize sustainability, they are sending a clear message to those companies that sustainability is important to them. This can incentivize companies to adopt more sustainable practices to attract ethical investors and remain competitive.

In addition, ethical investing can also have a positive impact on society. Investing in companies prioritizing social responsibility can help support initiatives promoting social justice, human rights, and equality. This can help create a more just and equitable society where everyone can access the resources and opportunities needed to thrive.

Ethical investing is a powerful tool for promoting sustainability and social responsibility. Investing in companies prioritizing these values can help create a more sustainable and equitable future for all.

Ethical and impact investing are powerful tools for investors who want to align their values with their financial goals. By investing in companies that prioritize ESG factors and positively impact society and the environment, investors can help create a more sustainable and equitable world.

Chapter Summary

- Ethical investing involves investing in companies that align with an investor's values and beliefs.
- Impact investing seeks to actively create positive change in climate change, poverty, and inequality.
- Ethical investing models include negative screening, positive screening, and shareholder advocacy.
- Ethical investing can drive innovation by encouraging companies to adopt more sustainable and responsible practices.
- Ethical investing can promote sustainability by encouraging companies to adopt more responsible practices.

- Sustainable investing assets reached $30.7 trillion in 2018, a 34% increase from 2016.
- Analysts estimated the impact investing market to be $715 billion in 2020.
- Ethical and impact investing are powerful tools for investors who want to align their values with their financial goals.

12

IMPACT INVESTING AND THE FUTURE OF INVESTING

A hand holding a sapling, surrounded by symbols of progress and innovation, representing the power of impact investing to cultivate sustainable growth and build a better future.

Impact investing is a relatively new concept that has gained significant traction recently. It is an investment approach that seeks to generate both financial returns and positive social and environmental impact. As a result, impact investing has the potential to transform the way we invest and create a more sustainable and equitable future. In this chapter, we will explore the trends in impact investing, its impact on the global economy and the financial industry, and the role of investors and consumers in driving this movement forward.

Trends in Impact Investing

Impact investing has grown significantly in recent years, with assets under management reaching over $715 billion in 2020. This growth is driven by several trends, including the increasing demand for sustainable and socially responsible investments, the rise of impact-focused funds and platforms, and the growing awareness of the need to address global challenges such as climate change and inequality.

One of the key trends in impact investing is the focus on **measurable impact**. As a result, investors are increasingly looking for investments that can demonstrate a clear and measurable social or environmental impact. This has led to the development of impact measurements and management frameworks, such as the Impact Management Project and the Global Impact Investing Network's IRIS+ system.

Another trend is the rise of impact-focused funds and platforms. These funds and platforms are dedicated to investing in companies and projects with a positive social or environmental impact. Examples include the Global Impact Investing Network, the Impact Investing Institute, and the Impact Investment Exchange.

Impact investing is also becoming more mainstream, with traditional financial institutions and asset managers entering the space. This is driven by the increasing demand from clients for sustainable and socially responsible investments and the potential for financial returns.

However, there are also challenges to the growth of impact investing, such as the need for more standardization in impact measurement and management and the difficulty in finding suitable investment opportunities that meet both financial and impact criteria.

Impact Investing and the Global Economy

Impact investing can significantly address global challenges such as climate change, poverty, and inequality. By investing in companies and projects that have a positive social or environmental impact, impact investors can help to create a more sustainable and equitable future.

One area where impact investing can significantly impact is the transition to a **low-carbon economy**. By investing in renewable energy, energy efficiency, and other climate solutions, impact investors can help to accelerate the transition to a more sustainable energy system.

Impact investing can also help to address poverty and inequality by investing in companies and projects that provide access to basic services such as healthcare, education, and financial services. This can help to create more inclusive and equitable societies.

However, impact investing alone cannot solve these global challenges. It needs to be part of a broader effort that includes policy changes, technological innovation, and social and cultural shifts.

Impact Investing and the Financial Industry

Impact investing transforms the financial industry by creating new investment opportunities and changing investors' thinking about risk and return. It also drives innovation in impact measurement and management, creating new business models that combine financial and impact objectives.

Impact investing changes the financial industry by creating new investment opportunities. Impact investors invest in companies and projects that traditional investors may overlook, such as social enterprises and community development projects. This is creating new sources of capital for these types of organizations and helping to drive innovation and growth.

Impact investing is also changing the way investors think about risk and return. For example, impact investors are willing to accept lower financial returns in exchange for a positive social or environmental impact. This challenges the traditional view that financial returns are the only measure of investment success.

Finally, impact investing is driving innovation in impact measurement and management. Impact investors are developing new frameworks and tools to measure and manage their investments' social and environmental impact. This is helping to create a more standardized and transparent approach to impact investing.

Impact Investing and the Role of Investors

Investors play a critical role in driving the growth of impact investing. They can use their capital to support companies and projects with a positive social or environmental impact and advocate for policy changes that support impact investing.

Investors can support impact investing by investing in impact-focused funds and platforms. These funds and platforms are dedicated to investing in companies and projects with a positive social or environmental impact. By investing in these funds and platforms, investors can support impact investing growth and help create a more sustainable and equitable future.

Investors can also advocate for policy changes that support impact investing. This can include changes to tax policies, regulations, and government procurement policies supporting impact investing growth.

Finally, investors can use their influence to encourage companies to adopt more sustainable and socially responsible practices. This can include engaging with companies on climate change, human rights, and diversity and inclusion issues.

Impact Investing and the Role of Consumers

Consumers also play a critical role in driving the growth of impact investing. They can use their purchasing power to support companies with a positive social or environmental impact and advocate for policy changes that support impact investing.

Consumers can support impact investing by buying products and services from companies with a positive social or environmental impact. This can include products made from sustainable materials or services that support local communities.

Consumers can also advocate for policy changes that support impact investing. This can include changes to tax policies, regulations, and government procurement policies supporting impact investing growth.

Finally, consumers can use their influence to encourage companies to adopt more sustainable and socially responsible practices. This can include engaging with companies on climate change, human rights, and diversity and inclusion issues.

Impact investing can transform our investment and create a more sustainable and equitable future. It is driven by several trends, including the increasing demand for sustainable and socially responsible investments, the rise of impact-focused funds and platforms, and the growing awareness of the need to address global challenges such as climate change and inequality. However, there are also challenges to the growth of impact investing, such as the need for more standardization in impact measurement and management and the difficulty in finding suitable investment opportunities that meet both financial and impact criteria. In addition, investors and consumers play a critical role in driving the growth of impact investing. By working together, we can create a more sustainable and equitable future.

Chapter Summary

- Impact investing has grown significantly in recent years, driven by the increasing demand for sustainable and socially responsible investments.
- The focus on measurable impact and the rise of impact-focused funds and platforms are key trends in impact investing.
- Impact investing has the potential to address global challenges such as climate change, poverty, and inequality.
- Impact investing transforms the financial industry by creating new investment opportunities and changing investors' thinking about risk and return.
- Investors can support impact investing by investing in impact-focused funds and platforms and advocating for policy changes that support impact investing.
- Consumers can support impact investing by buying products and services from companies with a positive social or environmental impact and advocating for policy changes supporting impact investing.
- Impact investing faces challenges like more standardization in impact measurement and management.
- Impact investing must be part of a broader effort that includes policy changes, technological innovation, and social and cultural shifts to address global challenges.

13

IMPACT INVESTING RESOURCES

A hand planting a seedling in a pot, symbolizing the potential of impact investing to foster sustainable agriculture and food systems, which are critical for achieving the Sustainable Development Goals related to hunger and poverty.

Impact investing is a rapidly growing field that attracts investors who want to impact society while earning a financial return positively. However, finding the right resources to navigate this complex field can be challenging. This chapter will explore the top impact investing organizations, publications, conferences, events, networks, communities, and tools that can help you make informed investment decisions and maximize your impact.

Impact Investing Organizations

Impact investing organizations are dedicated to promoting and facilitating impact investing. They provide various services, including research, education, networking, and investment opportunities. Here are five of the top impact investing organizations:

1. **Global Impact Investing Network (GIIN):** The GIIN is a nonprofit organization that works to increase the scale and effectiveness of impact investing. They provide research, tools, and resources to help investors and organizations make informed investment decisions.
2. **ImpactAssets:** ImpactAssets is a nonprofit organization that offers impact investing solutions for individuals, families, and institutions. They provide access to various impact investment opportunities, including private debt and equity, public equity, and fixed income.
3. **Acumen:** Acumen is a nonprofit organization that invests in companies working to solve some of the world's most pressing social and environmental problems. They provide patient capital, management support, and strategic advice to help these companies grow and succeed.
4. **B Lab:** B Lab is a nonprofit organization that certifies companies that meet rigorous social and environmental performance standards, accountability, and transparency.

They also provide tools and resources to help companies measure and improve their impact.

5. **Toniic:** Toniic is a global network of impact investors committed to using their capital to create positive social and environmental change. They provide various services, including education, networking, and investment opportunities.

Impact Investing Publications:

Impact investing publications provide valuable insights and information about the field's latest trends, best practices, and success stories. Here are five of the top impact investing publications:

1. **ImpactAlpha:** ImpactAlpha is a digital media platform that covers the latest news and trends in impact investing. They provide in-depth analysis, expert commentary, and various resources for impact investors.
2. **Stanford Social Innovation Review (SSIR):** SSIR is a quarterly magazine that covers the latest trends and best practices in social innovation and impacts investing. They provide insights from leading experts, case studies, and practical tools for social entrepreneurs and impact investors.
3. **NextBillion:** NextBillion is a digital media platform that covers the latest news and trends in social entrepreneurship, impact investing, and sustainable business. They provide insights from leading experts, case studies, and practical tools for social entrepreneurs and impact investors.
4. **Impact Investing Insights:** Impact Investing Insights is a monthly newsletter that provides insights and analysis on the latest trends and best practices in impact investing. They cover various topics, including impact measurement, social entrepreneurship, and sustainable finance.
5. **The Economist:** The Economist is a weekly magazine covering the latest business, finance, and economics news

and trends. They provide in-depth analysis and expert commentary on the impact investing landscape.

Impact Investing Conferences and Events

Impact investing conferences and events provide valuable opportunities to network with other impact investors, learn about the latest trends and best practices, and explore new investment opportunities. Here are five of the top impact investing conferences and events:

1. **SOCAP:** SOCAP is an annual conference that brings together impact investors, social entrepreneurs, and other stakeholders to explore new investment opportunities and share best practices. They provide a range of sessions, workshops, and networking opportunities.
2. **Skoll World Forum:** The Skoll World Forum is an annual conference that brings together social entrepreneurs, impact investors, and other stakeholders to explore new solutions to the world's most pressing social and environmental problems. They provide a range of sessions, workshops, and networking opportunities.
3. **Global Impact Investing Network Investor Forum:** The GIIN Investor Forum is an annual conference that gathers impact investors worldwide to share best practices, explore new investment opportunities, and build relationships.
4. **Social Finance Forum:** The Social Finance Forum is an annual conference that brings together impact investors, social entrepreneurs, and other stakeholders to explore new solutions to social and environmental problems. They provide a range of sessions, workshops, and networking opportunities.
5. **Impact Summit:** The Impact Summit is an annual conference that brings together impact investors, social entrepreneurs, and other stakeholders to explore new investment opportunities and share best practices. They

provide a range of sessions, workshops, and networking opportunities.

Impact Investing Networks and Communities:

Impact investing networks and communities provide valuable opportunities to connect with other impact investors, share best practices, and explore new investment opportunities. Here are five of the top impact investing networks and communities:

1. **Impact Hub:** Impact Hub is a global network of coworking spaces dedicated to promoting social and environmental impact. They provide various services, including networking events, workshops, and mentorship programs.
2. **Toniic:** Toniic is a global network of impact investors committed to using their capital to create positive social and environmental change. They provide various services, including education, networking, and investment opportunities.
3. **Social Venture Circle:** Social Venture Circle is a network of impact investors, social entrepreneurs, and other stakeholders committed to using business as a force for good. They provide various services, including networking events, mentorship programs, and investment opportunities.
4. **Investors' Circle:** Investors' Circle is a network of impact investors committed to using their capital to create positive social and environmental change. They provide various services, including networking events, mentorship programs, and investment opportunities.
5. **Confluence Philanthropy:** Confluence Philanthropy is a network of impact investors and philanthropists committed to using their capital to create positive social and environmental change. They provide various services, including networking events, educational programs, and investment opportunities.

Impact Investing Tools and Resources:

Impact investing tools and resources provide valuable insights and information to help investors make informed investment decisions and maximize their impact. Here are five of the top impact investing tools and resources:

1. **ImpactBase:** ImpactBase is a global database of impact investment funds, products, and services. It provides investors various tools and resources to help them identify and evaluate impact investment opportunities.
2. **IRIS:** IRIS is a set of standardized metrics used to measure impact investments' social, environmental, and financial performance. It provides investors a common language for measuring impact and comparing investment opportunities.
3. **GIIRS:** GIIRS is a rating system used to assess companies' and funds' social and environmental impact. It provides investors with a standardized way to evaluate the impact of their investments and compare investment opportunities.
4. **B Analytics:** B Analytics is a platform that provides companies with tools and resources to measure and improve their social and environmental impact. It also provides investors a way to evaluate the impact of their investments in certified B Corporations.
5. **Impact Investing Handbook:** The Impact Investing Handbook is a comprehensive guide to impact investing. It provides investors with practical tools and resources to help them make informed investment decisions and maximize their impact.

Impact investing is a powerful tool for creating positive social and environmental change while earning a financial return. Investors can make informed investment decisions and maximize their impact by leveraging the resources provided by impact investing organizations, publications, conferences, events, networks, communities, and tools. Whether you are a seasoned impact investor or just getting started, these resources can help you achieve your goals and make a difference in the world.

Chapter Summary

- Impact investing organizations provide research, education, networking, and investment opportunities.
- Impact investing publications provide insights and information about the field's latest trends, best practices, and success stories.
- Impact investing conferences and events provide valuable opportunities to network, learn, and explore new investment opportunities.
- Impact investing networks and communities provide valuable opportunities to connect with other impact investors, share best practices, and explore new investment opportunities.
- Impact investing tools and resources provide valuable insights and information to help investors make informed investment decisions and maximize their impact.
- The Global Impact Investing Network, ImpactAlpha, SOCAP, Impact Hub, and ImpactBase are among the top impact investing resources.
- IRIS, GIIRS, B Analytics, the Impact Investing Handbook, and the Skoll World Forum are among the top impact investing tools and resources.
- By leveraging these resources, investors can make informed investment decisions and maximize their impact.

EPILOGUE

As we come to the end of this book, it is important to reflect on the key takeaways and implications of impact investing. Impact investing is a powerful tool that combines financial returns with social and environmental impact. It can transform how we invest and create positive change in the world.

Summary of Impact Investing

Impact investing is a rapidly growing field that seeks to generate measurable social and environmental impact alongside financial returns. It is driven by a desire to address pressing global challenges such as poverty, inequality, climate change, and access to healthcare and education. Impact investors use various strategies and approaches to achieve their goals, including socially responsible investing, community investing, microfinance, and impact bonds.

Impact Investing and Social Change

Impact investing has the potential to create significant social change by directing capital toward businesses and organizations that are working to solve social and environmental problems. By investing in these organizations, impact investors can help to create jobs, improve access to essential services, and promote sustainable development. Impact investing can also shift the financial industry's focus towards more socially responsible and sustainable practices.

Impact Investing and the Future of the World

The world's future depends on our ability to address our complex social and environmental challenges. Impact investing can be critical in this effort by directing capital towards solutions that create positive social and environmental impact. In addition, by investing in businesses and organizations working to address these challenges, impact investors can help create a more sustainable and equitable future for all.

Impact Investing and You

Impact investing is not just for institutional investors or high-net-worth individuals. Anyone can become an impact investor by directing their investments towards businesses and organizations that align with their values and goals. Whether investing in a community development fund, supporting a social enterprise, or investing in renewable energy, your investments can make a difference.

Final Thoughts on Impact Investing

In conclusion, impact investing is a powerful tool that can help to create positive social and environmental impact while generating financial returns. It has the potential to transform the financial industry and create a more sustainable and equitable future for all. As you consider your investments, we encourage you to explore the world of impact investing and discover how you can make a difference.

ACKNOWLEDGMENTS

Writing a book is a journey; I could not have done it alone. So I want to express my deepest gratitude to the many people who have helped me along the way.

First and foremost, I would like to thank my family for their unwavering support and encouragement throughout the writing of this book. Their love and patience have been a constant source of inspiration; I could not have done this without them.

I also extend my deepest gratitude to my mentor Justina, whose guidance and wisdom have been invaluable in shaping my understanding of ESG and impact investing. Her insights and expertise have been instrumental in the development of this book.

I am also grateful to the team at Book Bound Studios for their support and guidance throughout the publishing process. The cover and interior design work provided by the team were amazing and exceeded my expectations.

I would also like to thank the many experts and practitioners in the field of impact investing who have shared their time and knowledge with me. Their insights and experiences have been invaluable in the development of this book.

Finally, thank you, the reader, for your interest in this topic. I hope this book will be a valuable resource for those looking to understand and implement impact strategies in their investment decisions.

Thank you all for your support and encouragement.

ABOUT THE AUTHOR

Robert Buckley is a financial professional with over 15 years of experience in the industry. He is a specialist in ESG and impact investing and has spent the past decade researching and studying the field. He has held various positions in the investment management sector, including portfolio management, research, and strategy development.

Robert is passionate about promoting sustainable and responsible investing and is dedicated to helping investors understand the benefits and risks of incorporating ESG factors in their investment decisions. He believes that by considering ESG factors, investors can achieve both financial returns and positively impact the world.

Robert enjoys hiking, reading, and spending time with his family in his free time.

Made in the USA
Monee, IL
04 November 2026

67383016R00115